THE SECOND
MRS. TANQUERAY

A Play in Four Acts

BY

ARTHUR W. PINERO

SAMUEL FRENCH

LONDON

NEW YORK   SYDNEY   TORONTO   HOLLYWOOD

Please see page iv for further copyright information

THE PERSONS OF THE PLAY

AUBREY TANQUERAY.
PAULA.
ELLEAN.
CAYLEY DRUMMLE.
MRS. CORTELYON.
CAPTAIN HUGH ARDALE.
GORDON JAYNE, M.D.
FRANK MISQUITH, Q.C., M.P.
SIR GEORGE ORREYED, BART.
LADY ORREYED.
MORSE.

The Present Day.

The Scene of the First Act is laid at Mr. Tanqueray's rooms, No. 2x The Albany, in the month of November; the occurrences of the succeeding Acts take place at his house, " Highercoombe," near Willowmere, Surrey, during the early part of the following year.

THE SECOND MRS. TANQUERAY

ACT I

SCENE.—AUBREY TANQUERAY'S *Chambers in the Albany—a richly and tastefully-decorated room. The wall* R. *is almost entirely taken up by a pair of doors which open into another room. Up* L., *at back, a small door supposed to lead to a bedchamber. At back* C., *a fireplace, with fire burning brightly. A luxurious easy chair on each side of the fireplace. On the* R. *of fireplace, against the wall, a writing-table and chair. On the writing-table, writing materials, a small cigar-cabinet and lighted spirit-lamp. On the* L. *wall, a heavy curtain drawn over a large window. Down* R.C., *set obliquely to face audience, a sofa. Down* L.C., *a circular table laid for a dinner which has reached the stage of dessert. On this table, wines in decanters, flowers, fruit, plate, silver, coffee-cups, etc., etc. Round the table, at equal distances, four chairs. Other articles of furniture, bric-à-brac, china, pictures, lamps, candles, etc., about the room. Everything to suggest wealth and refinement.*

AUBREY TANQUERAY, MISQUITH, *and* JAYNE *are seated at the dinner-table,* L.C. AUBREY *is forty-two, handsome, winning in manner, his speech and bearing retaining some of the qualities of young-manhood.* MISQUITH *is about forty-seven, genial and portly.* JAYNE *is a year or two* MISQUITH'S *senior; soft-speaking and precise—in appearance a type of the prosperous town physician.* MORSE, AUBREY'S *servant, takes the little cabinet of cigars and the spirit-lamp from table up* R.C., *places them beside* AUBREY, *and goes out door* R.

MISQUITH. Aubrey, it is a pleasant yet dreadful fact to contemplate, but it's nearly fifteen years since I first dined with you. You lodged in Piccadilly in those days, over a hat-shop. Jayne, I met you at that dinner, and Cayley Drummle.

JAYNE. Yes, yes. What a pity it is that Cayley isn't here to-night.

AUBREY. Confound the old gossip! His empty chair has been staring us in the face all through dinner. I ought to have told Morse to take it away.

MISQUITH. Odd, his sending no excuse.

AUBREY. I'll walk round to his lodgings later on and ask after him.

MISQUITH. I'll go with you.

5

JAYNE. So will I.

AUBREY (*opening the cigar-cabinet*). Doctor, it's useless to tempt you, I know. Frank——

(MISQUITH *and* AUBREY *smoke.*)

I particularly wished Cayley Drummle to be one of us to-night. You two fellows and Cayley are my closest, my best friends——

MISQUITH. My dear Aubrey !

JAYNE. I rejoice to hear you say so.

AUBREY. And I wanted to see the three of you round this table. You can't guess the reason.

MISQUITH. You desired to give us a most excellent dinner.

JAYNE. Obviously.

AUBREY (*hesitatingly*). Well—I—(*glancing at the clock*)—Cayley won't turn up now. (*He moves the candle from* R. *to* L. *of the table.*)

JAYNE. H'm, hardly.

AUBREY. Then you two shall hear it. Doctor, Frank, this is the last time we are to meet in these rooms.

JAYNE. The last time ?

MISQUITH. You're going to leave the Albany ?

AUBREY. Yes. You've heard me speak of a house I built in the country years ago, haven't you ?

MISQUITH. In Surrey.

AUBREY. Well, when my wife died I cleared out of that house and let it. I think of trying the place again.

MISQUITH. But you'll go raving mad if ever you find yourself down there alone.

AUBREY. Ah, but I shan't be alone, and that's what I wanted to tell you. I'm going to be married.

JAYNE. Going to be married ?

MISQUITH. Married ?

AUBREY. Yes—to-morrow.

JAYNE. To-morrow ?

MISQUITH. You take my breath away ! My dear fellow, I—I—of course, I congratulate you.

JAYNE. And—and so do I—heartily.

AUBREY. Thanks—thanks.

(*There is a moment or two of embarrassment.*)

MISQUITH. Er—ah—this is an excellent cigar.

JAYNE. Ah—um-—your coffee is remarkable.

AUBREY. Look here ; I daresay you two old friends think this treatment very strange, very unkind. So I want you to understand me. You know a marriage often cools friendships. What's the usual course of things ? A man's engagement is given out, he is congratulated, complimented upon his choice ; the church is filled with troops of friends, and he goes away happily to a chorus of good wishes. He comes back, sets up house in town or country, and thinks to resume the old associations, the old companionships. My dear Frank, my dear good doctor, it's very seldom that it can be done. Generally, a worm has begun to eat its way into those hearty, unreserved, prenuptial friendships ; a damnable constraint sets in and acts like a wasting disease ; and so, believe me, in nine cases out of ten a man's marriage severs for him more close ties than it forms.

MISQUITH. Well, my dear Aubrey, I earnestly hope——

AUBREY. I know what you're going to say, Frank. I hope so, too. In the meantime let's face dangers. I've reminded you of the *usual* course of things, but my marriage isn't even the conventional sort of marriage likely to satisfy society. Now, Cayley's a bachelor, but you two men have wives. By the by, my love to Mrs. Misquith and to Mrs. Jayne when you get home—don't forget that. Well, your wives may not—like—the lady I'm going to marry.

JAYNE. Aubrey, forgive me for suggesting that the lady you are going to marry may not like our wives—mine at least ; I beg your pardon, Frank.

AUBREY. Quite so ; then I must go the way my wife goes.

MISQUITH. Come, come, pray don't let us anticipate that either side will be called upon to make such a sacrifice.

AUBREY. Yes, yes, let us anticipate it. And let us make up our minds to have no slow bleeding-to-death of our friendship. We'll end a pleasant chapter here to-night, and after to-night start afresh. When my wife and I settle down at Willowmere it's possible that we shall all come together. But if this isn't to be, for Heaven's sake let us recognize that it is simply because it *can't* be, and not wear hypocritical faces and suffer and be wretched. Doctor, Frank —(*holding out his hands, one to* MISQUITH, *the other to* JAYNE)— good luck to all of us !

MISQUITH. But—but—do I understand we are to ask nothing ? Not even the lady's name, Aubrey ?

AUBREY. The lady, my dear Frank, belongs to the next chapter, and in that her name is Mrs. Aubrey Tanqueray.

JAYNE (*raising his coffee-cup*). Then, in an old-fashioned way, I propose a toast. Aubrey, Frank, I give you " The Next Chapter ! "

(*They drink the toast, saying,* " The Next Chapter ! ")

AUBREY. Doctor, find a comfortable chair ; Frank, you too. As we're going to turn out by and by, let me scribble a couple of notes now while I think of them.

MISQUITH }
JAYNE } (*together*). Certainly—yes, yes.

AUBREY. It might slip my memory when I get back.

(AUBREY *sits at the writing-table at the other end of the room, and writes.*)

JAYNE (*to* MISQUITH, *in a whisper*). Frank——

(MISQUITH *quietly leaves his chair and sits nearer to* JAYNE, *above table.*)

What is all this ? Simply a morbid crank of Aubrey's with regard to ante-nuptial acquaintances ?

MISQUITH. H'm ! Did you notice *one* expression he used ?

JAYNE. Let me think——

MISQUITH. " My marriage is not even the conventional sort of marriage likely to satisfy society."

JAYNE. Bless me, yes ! What does that suggest ?

MISQUITH. That he has a particular rather than a general reason for anticipating estrangement from his friends, I'm afraid.

JAYNE. A horrible *mésalliance* ! A dairymaid who has given him a glass of milk during a day's hunting, or a little anæmic shopgirl ! Frank, I'm utterly wretched !

MISQUITH. My dear Jayne, speaking in absolute confidence, I have never been more profoundly depressed in my life.

(MORSE *enters door* R.)

MORSE (*announcing*). Mr. Drummle.

(CAYLEY DRUMMLE *enters briskly.* MISQUITH *and* JAYNE *rise.* MORSE *retires.* DRUMMLE *is a neat little man of about five-and-forty, in manner bright, airy, debonair, but with an undercurrent of seriousness.*)

DRUMMLE. I'm in disgrace ; nobody realizes that more thoroughly than I do. Where's my host ?

AUBREY (*who has risen*). Cayley. (*He comes down* R.)

DRUMMLE (*shaking hands with him*). Don't speak to me till I have tendered my explanation. A harsh word from anybody would unman me.

(MISQUITH *and* JAYNE *shake hands with* DRUMMLE.)

AUBREY. Have you dined ?

DRUMMLE. No—unless you call a bit of fish, a cutlet, and a pancake dining.

AUBREY. Cayley, this is disgraceful.

JAYNE (*coming down* L.). Fish, a cutlet, and a pancake will require a great deal of explanation. (*He sits below the table.*)

MISQUITH. Especially the pancake. My dear friend, your case looks miserably weak.

DRUMMLE. Hear me ! hear me !

JAYNE. Now then !

MISQUITH. Come !

AUBREY. Well !

DRUMMLE. It so happens that to-night I was exceptionally *early* in dressing for dinner.

MISQUITH. For which dinner—the fish and cutlet?

DRUMMLE. For *this* dinner, of course—really, Frank! At a quarter to eight, in fact, I found myself trimming my nails, with ten minutes to spare. Just then enter my man with a note—would I hasten, as fast as cab could carry me, to old Lady Orreyed in Bruton Street?—" sad trouble." Now, recollect, please, I had ten minutes on my hands, old Lady Orreyed was a very dear friend of my mother's, and was in some distress.

AUBREY. Cayley, come to the fish and cutlet?

MISQUITH
JAYNE } *(together)*. Yes, yes, and the pancake!

DRUMMLE *(with mock indignation)*. Upon my word! Well, the scene in Bruton Street beggars description; the women servants looked scared, the men drunk; and there was poor old Lady Orreyed on the floor of her boudoir like Queen Bess among her pillows.

AUBREY. What's the matter?

DRUMMLE *(to everybody)*. You know George Orreyed?

MISQUITH. Yes.

JAYNE. I've met him.

DRUMMLE. Well, he's a thing of the past.

AUBREY. Not dead!

DRUMMLE. Certainly, in the worst sense. He's married Mabel Hervey.

MISQUITH. What!

DRUMMLE. It's true—this morning. The poor mother showed me his letter—a dozen curt words, and some of those ill-spelt.

MISQUITH *(walking up to the fireplace)*. I'm very sorry.

JAYNE. Pardon my ignorance—who *was* Mabel Hervey?

DRUMMLE. You don't——? Oh, of course not. *(He sits L.C.)* Miss Hervey—Lady Orreyed, as she now is—was a lady who would have been, perhaps had been, described in the reports of the Police or the Divorce Court as an actress. Had she belonged to a lower stratum of our advanced civilization she would, in the event of judicial inquiry, have defined her calling with equal justification as that of a dressmaker. To do her justice, she is a type of a class which is immortal. Physically, by the strange caprice of creation, curiously beautiful; mentally, she lacks even the strength of deliberate viciousness. *(He rises and moves c.)* Paint her portrait, it would symbolize a creature perfectly patrician; lance a vein of her superbly-modelled arm, you would get the poorest *vin ordinaire*! Her affections, emotions, impulses, her very existence—a burlesque! Flaxen, five-and-twenty, and feebly frolicsome; anybody's, in less gentle society I should say everybody's, property! That, Doctor, was Miss Hervey who is the new Lady Orreyed. Dost thou like the picture?

MISQUITH *(behind the table)*. Very good, Cayley! Bravo!

AUBREY *(rising and laying his hand on* DRUMMLE'S *shoulder)*. You'd scarcely believe it, Jayne, but none of us really know anything about this lady, our gay young friend here, I suspect, least of all.

DRUMMLE. Aubrey, I applaud your chivalry.

AUBREY. And perhaps you'll let me finish a couple of letters which Frank and Jayne have given me leave to write. (*Returning to the writing-table.*) Ring for what you want, like a good fellow !

(AUBREY *resumes his writing.*)

MISQUITH (*to* DRUMMLE). Still, the fish and cutlet remain unexplained.

DRUMMLE. Oh, the poor old woman was so weak that I insisted upon her taking some food, and felt there was nothing for it but to sit down opposite her. The fool! the blackguard!

MISQUITH (*going to settee and sitting*). Poor Orreyed ! Well, he's gone under for a time.

DRUMMLE. For a time ! My dear Frank, I tell you he has absolutely ceased to be.

(AUBREY, *who has been writing busily, turns his head towards the speakers and listens. His lips are set, and there is a frown upon his face.*)

For all practical purposes you may regard him as the late George Orreyed. To-morrow the very characteristics of his speech, as we remember them, will have become obsolete.

JAYNE. But surely, in the course of years, he and his wife will outlive——

DRUMMLE. No, no, Doctor, don't try to upset one of my settled beliefs. You may dive into many waters, but there is *one* social Dead Sea——!

JAYNE. Perhaps you're right.

DRUMMLE. Right ! Good God ! I wish you could prove me otherwise ! Why, for years I've been sitting, and watching and waiting.

MISQUITH. You're in form to-night, Cayley. May we ask where you've been in the habit of squandering your useful leisure ?

DRUMMLE. Where ? On the shore of that same sea.

MISQUITH. And, pray, what have you been waiting for ?

DRUMMLE. For some of my best friends *to come up.*

(AUBREY *utters a half-stifled exclamation of impatience; then he hurriedly gathers up his papers from the writing-table. The three men turn to him.*)

Eh ?

AUBREY (*pushing the chair in*). Oh, I—I'll finish my letters in the other room if you'll excuse me for five minutes. Tell Cayley the news.

(*He goes out* R.)

DRUMMLE (*hurrying to the door and speaking off*). My dear fellow, my jabbering has disturbed you! I'll never talk again as long as I live!

MISQUITH. Close the door, Cayley.

(DRUMMLE *shuts the door.*)

JAYNE. Cayley——

DRUMMLE (*advancing to the dinner table* C.). A smoke, a smoke, or I perish! (*He selects a cigar from the little cabinet.*)

(JAYNE *moves away from the table.*)

JAYNE. Cayley, marriages are in the air.

DRUMMLE. Are they? Discover the bacillus, Doctor, and destroy it.

JAYNE. I mean, among our friends.

DRUMMLE (*cutting his cigar*). Oh, Nugent Warrinder's engagement to Lady Alice Tring. I've heard of that. They're not to be married till the spring.

JAYNE. Another marriage that concerns us a little takes place to-morrow.

DRUMMLE. Whose marriage?

JAYNE. Aubrey's.

DRUMMLE. Aub——! (*Looking towards* MISQUITH.) Is it a joke?

MISQUITH (*standing* R.C.). No.

DRUMMLE (*walking slowly to* C., *looking from* MISQUITH *to* JAYNE). To whom?

MISQUITH. He doesn't tell us.

JAYNE. We three were asked here to-night to receive the announcement. Aubrey has some theory that marriage is likely to alienate a man from his friends, and it seems to me he has taken the precaution to wish us good-bye.

MISQUITH. No, no.

JAYNE. Practically, surely.

DRUMMLE (*thoughtfully*). Marriage in general, does he mean, or *this* marriage?

JAYNE. That's the point. Frank says——

MISQUITH. No, no, no; I feared it suggested——

JAYNE. Well, well. (*To* DRUMMLE.) What do you think of it?

DRUMMLE (*after a slight pause*). Is there a light there?

(JAYNE *points to the spirit-lamp and walks up* L.C.)

(*Lighting his cigar.*) He—wraps the lady—in mystery—you say?

MISQUITH. Most modestly.

DRUMMLE. Aubrey's—not—a very—young man.

JAYNE (C.). Forty-three.

DRUMMLE. Ah! *L'age critique!*

MISQUITH. A dangerous age—yes, yes.

DRUMMLE. When you two fellows go home, do you mind leaving me behind here ?

MISQUITH. Not at all.

JAYNE. By all means.

DRUMMLE. All right. (*Anxiously*.) Deuce take it, the man's second marriage mustn't be another mistake ! (*With his head bent he walks up to the fireplace.*)

JAYNE. You knew him in his short married life, Cayley. Terribly unsatisfactory, wasn't it ?

DRUMMLE. Well—— (*Looking at the door* R.) I quite closed that door ?

MISQUITH. Yes.

(*He settles himself on the top end of the sofa ;* JAYNE *is seated in an armchair.*)

DRUMMLE (*smoking, with his back to the fire*). He married a Miss Herriott ; that was in the year eighteen—confound dates—twenty years ago. She was a lovely creature—by Jove, she was ; by religion a Roman Catholic. She was one of your cold sort, you know—all marble arms and black velvet. I remember her with painful distinctness as the only woman who ever made me nervous.

MISQUITH (*softly*). Ha, ha !

DRUMMLE. He loved her—to distraction, as they say. (*Glancing towards the door.*) Jupiter, how fervently that poor devil courted her ! But I don't believe she allowed him even to squeeze her fingers. She *was* an iceberg ! As for kissing, the mere contact would have given him chapped lips. However, he married her and took her away, the latter greatly to my relief.

JAYNE. Abroad, you mean ?

DRUMMLE. Eh ? Yes. I imagine he gratified her by renting a villa in Lapland, but I don't know. After awhile they returned, and then I saw how woefully Aubrey had miscalculated results.

JAYNE. Miscalculated——?

DRUMMLE. He had reckoned, poor wretch, that in the early days of marriage she would thaw. But she didn't. I used to picture him closing his doors and making up the fire in the hope of seeing her features relax. Bless her, the thaw never set in ! I believe she kept a thermometer in her stays and always registered ten degrees below zero. However, in time a child came—a daughter.

JAYNE. Didn't that——?

DRUMMLE. Not a bit of it ; it made matters worse. Frightened at her failure to stir up in him some sympathetic religious belief, she determined upon strong measures with regard to the child. He opposed her for a miserable year or so, but she wore him down, and the insensible little brat was placed in a convent, first in France, then in Ireland. Not long afterwards the mother died (*he comes down*) strangely enough, of fever, the only warmth, I believe, that ever came to that woman's body.

MISQUITH. Don't, Cayley! (*He rises and slowly moves up* R.C.)

JAYNE. The child is living, we know.

DRUMMLE. Yes, if you choose to call it living. Miss Tanqueray —a young woman of nineteen now—is in the Loretto convent at Armagh. She professes to have found her true vocation in a religious life, and within a month or two will take final vows. (*He goes down* R.C. *and sits on the sofa.*)

MISQUITH. He ought to have removed his daughter from the convent when the mother died. (*He moves to front of the fire* C.)

DRUMMLE. Yes, yes, but absolutely at the end there was reconciliation between husband and wife, and she won his promise that the child should complete her conventual education. He reaped his reward. When he attempted to gain his girl's confidence and affection he was too late ; he found he was dealing with the spirit of the mother. You remember his visit to Ireland last month ?

JAYNE. Yes.

DRUMMLE. That was to wish his girl good-bye.

MISQUITH. Poor fellow !

DRUMMLE. He sent for me when he came back. I think he must have had a lingering hope that the girl would relent—would come to life, as it were—at the last moment, for, for an hour or so, in this room, he was terribly shaken. I'm sure he'd clung to that hope from the persistent way in which he kept breaking off in his talk to repeat one dismal word, as if he couldn't realize his position without dinning this damned word into his head.

JAYNE. What word was that ?

DRUMMLE. Alone—alone.

(AUBREY *enters* R.)

AUBREY (*advancing to the fire*). A thousand apologies !

DRUMMLE (*gaily*). We are talking about you, my dear Aubrey.

(*During the telling of the story,* MISQUITH *has risen and gone to the fire, and* DRUMMLE *has thrown himself full length on the sofa.* AUBREY *now joins* MISQUITH *and* JAYNE.)

AUBREY (*between* MISQUITH *and* JAYNE). Well, Cayley, are you surprised ?

DRUMMLE. Surp——! I haven't been surprised for twenty years.

AUBREY. And you're not angry with me ?

DRUMMLE. Angry ! (*Rising.*) Because you considerately withhold the name of a lady with whom it is now the object of my life to become acquainted ? My dear fellow, you pique my curiosity, you give zest to my existence ! And as for a wedding, who on earth wants to attend that familiar and probably draughty function ? Ugh ! (*Crossing to the table* L.C.) My cigar's out.

AUBREY (*walking down* R.C.). Let's talk about something else.
MISQUITH (*coming down, looking at his watch*). Not to-night,
Aubrey.

AUBREY. My dear Frank!

MISQUITH. I go up to Scotland to-morrow, and there are some
little matters——

JAYNE. I am off too.

AUBREY. No, no.

JAYNE. I must : I have to give a look to a case in Clifford Street
on my way home.

AUBREY (*going to the door* R.). Well!

(MISQUITH *and* JAYNE *exchange looks with* DRUMMLE.)

(*Opening the door and calling.*) Morse, hats and coats! (*Return-
ing.*) I shall write to you all next week from Genoa or Florence.
Now, Doctor, Frank, remember, my love to Mrs. Misquith and to
Mrs. Jayne!

(MORSE *enters* R. *with hats and coats. He gives* MISQUITH'S *first, then*
DRUMMLE'S, *then* JAYNE'S.)

MISQUITH⎫
JAYNE   ⎬(*together*). Yes, yes—yes, yes.

AUBREY. And your young people!

(*As* MISQUITH *and* JAYNE *put on their coats there is the clatter of
careless talk.*)

JAYNE. Cayley, I meet you at dinner on Sunday.

DRUMMLE. At the Stratfields'. That's very pleasant.

MISQUITH (*putting on his coat with* AUBREY'S *aid*). Ah-h!

AUBREY. What's wrong?

MISQUITH. A twinge. Why didn't I go to Aix in August?

JAYNE (*shaking hands with* DRUMMLE). Good night, Cayley.

DRUMMLE. Good night, my dear Doctor!

MISQUITH (*shaking hands with* DRUMMLE). Cayley, are you in
town for long?

DRUMMLE. Dear friend, I'm nowhere for long. Good night.

MISQUITH. Good night.

(AUBREY, JAYNE *and* MISQUITH *go out, followed by* MORSE ; *the
hum of talk is continued outside.*)

AUBREY. A cigar, Frank?

MISQUITH. No, thank you.

AUBREY. Going to walk, Doctor?

JAYNE. If Frank will.

MISQUITH. By all means.

AUBREY. It's a cold night.

(*The door is closed by* MORSE. DRUMMLE *remains standing* L.C. *with
his coat on his arm and his hat in his hand. The slam of the street
door is heard off* R.)

DRUMMLE (*to himself, thoughtfully*). Now then ! What the devil——!

(*After a short silence,* AUBREY *returns.*)

AUBREY (*eyeing* DRUMMLE *a little awkwardly*). Well, Cayley ?
DRUMMLE. Well, Aubrey ?

(AUBREY *walks up to the fire and stands looking into it.* DRUMMLE *crosses to* R.C.)

AUBREY. You're not going, old chap ?

(DRUMMLE *deliberately puts his hat and coat on the sofa and sits.*)

DRUMMLE. No.
AUBREY (*after a slight pause, with a forced laugh*). Hah ! Cayley, I never thought I should feel—shy—with you. (*Going to fireplace.*)
DRUMMLE (*shortly*). Why do you ?
AUBREY. Never mind. (*Turns to fire.*)
DRUMMLE. Now, I can quite understand a man wishing to be married in the dark, as it were.
AUBREY. You can ?
DRUMMLE (*argumentatively*). In your place I should very likely adopt the same course.
AUBREY. You think so ?
DRUMMLE. And if I intended marrying a lady not prominently in Society, as I presume you do—as I presume you do——
AUBREY. Well ?
DRUMMLE. As I presume you do, I'm not sure that *I* should tender her for preliminary dissection at afternoon tea-tables.
AUBREY. No ?
DRUMMLE. In fact, there is probably only one person—were I in your position to-night—with whom I should care to chat the matter over.
AUBREY. Who's that ?
DRUMMLE. Yourself, of course. (*Going to* AUBREY *and standing beside him.*) Of course, yourself, old friend.
AUBREY (*after a pause*). I must seem a brute to you, Cayley. But there are some acts which are hard to explain, hard to defend——
DRUMMLE. To defend——?
AUBREY. Some acts which one must trust to time to put right. (*He sits* L.C.)

(DRUMMLE *watches him for a moment, then takes up his hat and coat.*)

DRUMMLE. Well, I'll be moving.
AUBREY. Cayley ! Confound you and your old friendship ! Do you think I forget it ? Put your coat down ! Why did you stay behind here ? Cayley, the lady I am going to marry is the lady—who is known as—Mrs. Jarman.

(*There is a pause.*)

DRUMMLE (*in a low voice*). Mrs. Jarman! are you serious? (*He walks up to the fireplace, where he leans upon the mantelpiece, uttering something like a groan.*)

AUBREY (*starting up*). As you've got this out of me I give you leave to say all you care to say. Come, we'll be plain with each other. (*Crossing to* R.C.) You know Mrs. Jarman?

DRUMMLE (*coming down* L.C., *facing him*). I first met her at—what does it matter?

AUBREY. Yes, yes, everything! Come!

DRUMMLE. I met her at Homburg, two—three seasons ago.

(*The next few lines are spoken very quickly.*)

AUBREY. *Not* as Mrs. Jarman?

DRUMMLE. No.

AUBREY. She was then——?

DRUMMLE. Mrs. Dartry.

AUBREY. Yes. She has also seen you in London, she says.

DRUMMLE. Certainly.

AUBREY. In Aldford Street. Go on.

DRUMMLE (*with an entreative motion of his hands*). Please!

AUBREY. I insist.

DRUMMLE (*with a slight shrug of the shoulders*). Some time last year I was asked by a man to sup at his house, one night after the theatre.

AUBREY. Mr. Selwyn Ethurst—a bachelor.

DRUMMLE. Yes.

AUBREY. You were surprised therefore to find Mr. Ethurst aided in his cursed hospitality by a lady.

DRUMMLE. I was unprepared.

AUBREY. The lady you had known as Mrs. Dartry?

(DRUMMLE *inclines his head silently.* AUBREY *restlessly moves across to up* L.C., *then comes down again to* R.C.)

There is something of a yachting cruise in the Mediterranean too, is there not?

DRUMMLE. I joined Peter Jarman's yacht at Marseilles, in the spring, a month before he died.

AUBREY. Mrs. Jarman was on board?⎞
DRUMMLE. She was a kind hostess. ⎟
AUBREY. And an old acquaintance? ⎬ (*Quickly.*)
DRUMMLE. Yes. ⎟
AUBREY. You have told your story. ⎠

DRUMMLE. With your assistance.

AUBREY. I have put you to the pain of telling it to show you that this is not the case of a blind man entrapped by an artful woman. Let me add that Mrs. Jarman has no legal right to that name, that she is simply Miss Ray—Miss Paula Ray. (*He walks away from* DRUMMLE *and sits up* L.C.)

DRUMMLE (*crossing to the sofa and picking up his coat*). I should like to express my regret, Aubrey, for the way in which I spoke of George Orreyed's marriage.

AUBREY. You mean you compare Lady Orreyed with Miss Ray ?

(DRUMMLE *is silent.*)

(*Coming down towards* DRUMMLE, *hotly.*) Oh, of course ! To you, Cayley, all women who have been roughly treated, and who dare to survive by borrowing a little of our philosophy, are alike. You see in the crowd of the Ill-used only one pattern ; you can't detect the shades of goodness, intelligence, even nobility there. Well, how should you ? The crowd is dimly lighted ! And, besides, yours is the way of the world. (*He sits* L.C.)

DRUMMLE. My dear Aubrey, I *live* in the world. (*He throws his hat and coat back.*)

AUBREY. The name we give our little parish of St. James's.

DRUMMLE (*crossing to* C.). And you are quite prepared, my friend, to forfeit the esteem of your little parish ?

AUBREY. I avoid mortification by shifting from one parish to another. I give up Pall Mall for the Surrey hills ; leave off varnishing my boots and double the thickness of the soles.

DRUMMLE. And your skin—do you double the thickness of that also ?

AUBREY. I know you think me a fool, Cayley—you needn't infer that I'm a coward into the bargain. No ! I know what I'm doing, and I do it deliberately, defiantly. I'm alone ; I injure no living soul by the step I'm going to take ; and so you can't urge the one argument which might restrain me. (*He rises, moves slowly down* L. *and sits in the chair in front of the table.*) Of course, I don't expect you to think compassionately, fairly even, of the woman whom I—whom I am drawn to——

DRUMMLE. My dear Aubrey, I assure you I consider Mrs.— Miss Jarman—Mrs. Ray—Miss Ray—delightful. But I confess there is a form of chivalry which I gravely distrust, especially in a man of—our age.

AUBREY. Thanks. I've heard you say that from forty till fifty a man is at heart either a stoic or a satyr.

DRUMMLE (*protestingly*). Ah ! now——

AUBREY. I am neither. I have a temperate, honourable affection for Mrs. Jarman. She has never met a man who has treated her well—I intend to treat her well. That's all. And in a few years, Cayley, if you've not quite forsaken me, I'll prove to you that it's possible to rear a life of happiness, of good repute, on a—miserable foundation.

DRUMMLE (*offering his hand*). Do prove it !

AUBREY (*taking his hand*). We have spoken too freely of—of Mrs. Jarman. I was excited—angry. Please forget it !

DRUMMLE. My dear Aubrey, when we next meet I shall remember nothing but my respect for the lady who bears your name.

(MORSE *enters, closing the door, R., behind him carefully.*)

AUBREY. What is it?

MORSE (*hesitatingly*). May I speak to you, sir?

(DRUMMLE *wanders away up L., looking at the pictures.*)

(*In an undertone.*) Mrs. Jarman, sir.

AUBREY (*softly to* MORSE). Mrs. Jarman! Do you mean she is at the lodge in her carriage?

MORSE. No, sir—here. (AUBREY *looks towards* DRUMMLE, *perplexed.*) There's a nice fire in your—in that room, sir. (*Glancing in the direction of the door leading to the bedroom.*)

AUBREY (*between his teeth, angrily*). Very well.

(MORSE *retires.* AUBREY *moves up back of the sofa. Hearing the door close,* DRUMMLE *comes down.*)

DRUMMLE (*looking at his watch*). A quarter to eleven—horrible! (*Crossing to sofa and taking up his hat and coat.*) Must get to bed —up late every night this week.

(AUBREY *assists* DRUMMLE *with his coat, standing on his L.; and as he does so he looks towards the door up L., listening.*)

Thank you. Well, good night, Aubrey. I feel I've been dooced serious, quite out of keeping with myself; pray overlook it.

AUBREY (*kindly*). Ah, Cayley!

DRUMMLE. And remember that, after all, I'm merely a spectator in life; nothing more than a man at a play, in fact; only, like the old-fashioned playgoer, I love to see certain characters happy and comfortable at the finish. You understand? (*He delivers this speech with much surface gaiety, to hide deeper emotion.*)

AUBREY. I think I do.

DRUMMLE. Then, for as long as you can, old friend, will you— keep a stall for me?

AUBREY. Yes, Cayley.

DRUMMLE (*gaily*). Ah, ha! Good night! (*Bustling to the door.*) Don't bother! I'll let myself out! Good night! God bless yer!

(*He goes out;* AUBREY *follows him. The stage is empty for a moment, then* MORSE *enters by the other door up L., carrying some unopened letters which after a little consideration he places on the mantelpiece against the clock.* AUBREY *returns, walking across to L.C.* MORSE *goes to the door R., and stands waiting.*)

AUBREY. Yes?

MORSE. You hadn't seen your letters that came by the nine o'clock post, sir; I've put 'em where they'll catch your eye by and by.

AUBREY. Thank you.

MORSE (*hesitatingly.*) Gunter's cook and waiter have gone, sir. Would you prefer me to go to bed?

AUBREY (*frowning*). Certainly not.

MORSE. Very well, sir.

(*He goes out.*)

AUBREY (*opening the upper door* L.). Paula! Paula! (*He goes* C.)

(PAULA *enters and throws her arms round his neck. She is a young woman of about twenty-seven : beautiful, fresh, innocent-looking. She is in superb evening dress.*)

PAULA. Dearest!

AUBREY. Why have you come here?

PAULA (*drawing back*). Angry?

AUBREY. Yes—no. But it's eleven o'clock. (*He shuts the door.*)

PAULA (*laughing*). I know. (*Watching him.*)

AUBREY. What on earth will Morse think? (*He returns.*)

PAULA. Do you trouble yourself about what servants *think*?

AUBREY. Of course.

PAULA. Goose! They're only machines made to wait upon people—and to give evidence in the Divorce Court. (*Looking round.*) Oh, indeed! A snug little dinner!

AUBREY (*lightly*). Three men.

PAULA (*suspiciously*). Men?

AUBREY (*decisively*). Men.

PAULA (*penitently*). Ah! (*Sitting* R. *of the table.*) I'm so hungry.

AUBREY. Let me get you some game pie, or some—— (*He moves to back of the table, as if going to the sideboard* L.)

PAULA. No, no, hungry for this. What beautiful fruit! I love fruit when it's expensive.

(*He clears a space on the table, places a plate before her, and helps her to fruit.*)

I haven't dined, Aubrey dear.

AUBREY. My poor girl! Why?

PAULA. In the first place, I forgot to order any dinner, and my cook, who has always loathed me, thought he'd pay me out before he departed.

AUBREY. The beast!

PAULA. That's precisely what I——

AUBREY. No, Paula!

PAULA. What I told my maid to call him. What next will you think of me?

AUBREY (*sitting above the table*). Forgive me. You must be starved.

PAULA (*eating fruit*). *I* didn't care. As there was nothing to eat, I sat in my best frock, with my toes on the dining-room fender, and dreamt, oh, such a lovely dinner-party.

AUBREY. Dear lonely little woman!

PAULA. It was perfect. I saw you at the end of a very long table, opposite me, and we exchanged sly glances now and again over the flowers. We were host and hostess, Aubrey, and had been married about five years.

AUBREY (*kissing her hand*). Five years.

PAULA. And on each side of us was the nicest set imaginable— you know, dearest, the sort of men and women that can't be imitated.

AUBREY. Yes, yes. Eat some more fruit.

PAULA. But I haven't told you the best part of my dream.

AUBREY. Tell me.

PAULA. Well, although we had been married only such a few years, I seemed to know by the look on their faces that none of our guests had ever heard anything—anything—anything peculiar about the fascinating hostess.

AUBREY (*bending over her*). That's just how it will be, Paula. The world moves so quickly. That's just how it will be.

PAULA (*with a little grimace*). I wonder! (*Glancing at the fire.*) Ugh! do throw another log on.

AUBREY (*rising and mending the fire*). There. But you mustn't be here long.

PAULA. Hospitable wretch! I've something important to tell you. (*He makes towards her. She stops him.*) No, stay where you are. (*Turning from him, her face averted.*) Look here, that was my dream, Aubrey; but the fire went out while I was dozing, and I woke up with a regular fit of the shivers. And the result of it all was that I ran upstairs and scribbled you a letter.

AUBREY (*another movement*). Dear baby!

PAULA. Remain where you are. (*Taking a letter from her pocket.*) This is it. (*Rising.*) I've given you an account of myself, furnished you with a list of my adventures since I—you know. (*Weighing the letter in her hand.*) I wonder if it would go for a penny. Most of it you're acquainted with; *I've* told you a good deal, haven't I?

AUBREY. Oh, Paula!

PAULA. What I haven't told you I daresay you've heard from others. But in case they've omitted anything—the dears—it's all here.

AUBREY. Why in Heaven's name must you talk like this to-night?

PAULA. It may save discussion by and by, don't you think? (*Holding out the letter.*) There you are.

AUBREY. No, dear, no. (*He takes the letter.*)

PAULA (R.C.). Take it. Read it through after I've gone, and then—read it again, and turn the matter over in your mind finally. And if, even at the very last moment, you feel you—oughtn't to go to church with me, send a messenger to Pont Street, any time before eleven to-morrow, telling me that you're afraid, and I—I'll take the blow.

AUBREY (*quietly*). Why, what—what do you think I am?

PAULA. That's it. It's because I know you're such a dear good fellow that I want to save you the chance of ever feeling sorry you married me. I really love you so much, Aubrey, that to save you that I'd rather you treated me as—as the others have done.

AUBREY (*turning from her with a cry*). Oh!

PAULA (*after a slight pause*). I suppose I've shocked you. I can't help it if I have.

(*She sits R.C., with assumed languor and indifference. He turns to her.*)

AUBREY. My dearest, you don't understand me. I—I can't bear to hear you always talking about—what's done with. I tell you I'll never remember it ; Paula, can't you dismiss it ? Try. (*He kneels, impulsively, beside her.*) Darling, if we promise each other to forget, to forget, we're bound to be happy. After all, it's a mechanical matter ; the moment a wretched thought enters your head, you quickly think of something bright—it depends on one's will. (*Referring to the letter he holds in his hand.*) Shall I burn this, dear ? Let me, let me ! (*Rising.*)

PAULA (*with a shrug of the shoulders*). I don't suppose there's much that's new to you in it—just as you like.

(*He goes to the fire and burns the letter.*)

AUBREY. There's an end of it. (*Returning to her.*) What's the matter ?

PAULA (*rising, coldly*). Oh, nothing ! (*Going up L.C.*) I'll go and put my cloak on.

AUBREY (*detaining her*). What *is* the matter ?

PAULA (*pouting*). Well, I think you might have said, "You're very generous, Paula," or at least, "Thank you, dear," when I offered to set you free.

AUBREY (*catching her in his arms*). Ah !

PAULA. Ah ! ah ! Ha, ha ! It's all very well, but you don't know what it cost me to make such an offer. I do so want to be married.

AUBREY (*releasing her*). But you never imagined——?

PAULA. Perhaps not. And yet I *did* think of what I'd do at the end of our acquaintance if you had preferred to behave like the rest. (*Taking a flower from her bodice.*)

AUBREY. Hush !

PAULA (*indifferently*). Oh, I forgot !

AUBREY. What would you have done when we parted ?

PAULA (*matter of fact*). Why, killed myself.

AUBREY. Paula, dear !

PAULA. It's true. (*She goes to him, putting the flower in his buttonhole.*) Do you know I feel certain I should make away with myself if anything serious happened to me.

AUBREY. Anything serious! (*Blankly*.) What, has nothing ever been serious to you, Paula?

PAULA. Not lately; not since a long while ago. (*Impressively*.) I made up my mind then to have done with taking things seriously. If I hadn't, I—— However, we won't talk about that.

AUBREY. But now, now, life will be different to you, won't it —quite different? Eh, dear?

PAULA. Oh yes, now. (*Entreatively*.) Only, Aubrey, mind you keep me always happy.

AUBREY. I will try to.

PAULA. I know I couldn't swallow a second big dose of misery. I know that if ever I felt wretched again—truly wretched—I should take a leaf out of Connie Tirlemont's book. You remember? (*With a look of horror*.) They found her—— (*She suddenly stops and looks down, as if she saw the lady in her " mind's eye."*)

AUBREY. For God's sake, don't let your thoughts run on such things!

PAULA (*laughing*). Ha, ha, how scared you look! (*She goes up* L.C.; *then stops and looks at the clock*.) There, think of the time! Dearest, what will my coachman say! My cloak!

(*She runs off, gaily, by the upper door.* AUBREY *looks after her for a moment, then he walks up to the fire and stands warming his feet at the bars. As he does so he raises his head and observes the letters upon the mantelpiece. He takes one down quickly*.)

AUBREY. Ah! Ellean! (*Opening the letter with a knife which he finds upon the writing-table and reading in a low voice*.) " My dear father,—A great change has come over me. I believe my mother in Heaven has spoken to me, and counselled me to turn to you in your loneliness. At any rate, your words have reached my heart, and I no longer feel fitted for this solemn life. I am ready to take my place by you. Dear father, will you receive me?— ELLEAN."

(PAULA *re-enters, dressed in a handsome cloak. He stares at her as if he hardly realized her presence. She goes down stage and picks up gloves that she has previously placed on* L.C. *table. Surprised at his silence, she turns to him.* AUBREY *comes* R. *of her*.)

PAULA. What are you staring at? Don't you admire my cloak?

AUBREY. Yes.

PAULA (*petulantly*). Couldn't you wait till I'd gone before reading your letters?

AUBREY (*putting the letter away*). I beg your pardon.

PAULA. Take me downstairs to the carriage. (*Slipping her arm through his*.) How I tease you! To-morrow! I'm so happy!

(*They go out.*)

The CURTAIN *falls.*

ACT II

SCENE.—*A morning-room in* AUBREY TANQUERAY'S *house, "Higher-coombe," near Willowmere, Surrey—a bright and prettily furnished apartment of irregular shape. Down* R., *fireplace with fire burning. Up* R.C., *double doors opening into a small hall. Up* L.C., *a large recessed window through which is seen a view of extensive grounds. Down* L., *a door. Up* R., *a piano, open, and music-stool. Up* C., *a small table and two chairs. In the window-recess, a writing-table and library chair. On the blotting-book, an addressed letter stamped for the post. Down* R.C., *a circular table tastefully laid for breakfast —silver, flowers, fruit, etc. On the* R. *of this table, a settee to seat two persons; on the* L., *an armchair.* L.C., *a table; on the* L. *of this table, another settee to match its fellow. On the table, a newspaper. On the mantelpiece, a clock. Other articles of furniture to fill spaces—everything charming and tasteful.*

TIME.—*A morning in early spring. The sun streams in through the window.*

AUBREY *and* PAULA *are seated* R.C. *at breakfast, and* AUBREY *is silently reading his letters. Two servants, a man and a woman, hand dishes and then retire, door* R.C. *After a little while* AUBREY *puts his letters aside and looks across to the window.*

AUBREY. Sunshine! Spring!

PAULA (*glancing at the clock*). Exactly six minutes.

AUBREY. Six minutes?

PAULA. Six minutes, Aubrey dear, since you made your last remark.

AUBREY. I beg your pardon; I was reading my letters. Have you seen Ellean this morning?

PAULA (*coldly*). Your last observation but one was about Ellean.

AUBREY. Dearest, what *shall* I talk about?

PAULA. Ellean breakfasted two hours ago, Morgan tells me, and then went out walking with her dog.

AUBREY. She wraps up warmly, I hope; this sunshine is deceptive.

PAULA. I ran about the lawn last night, after dinner, in satin shoes. Were you anxious about me?

AUBREY. Certainly.

PAULA (*melting*). Really?

AUBREY. You make me wretchedly anxious; you delight in doing incautious things. You are incurable.

23

(*She rises and goes round back of the table to him.*)

PAULA. Ah, what a beast I am! (*Kissing him, then glancing at the letters by his side.*) A letter from Cayley?

AUBREY. He is staying very near here, with Mrs.—— Very near here.

PAULA (*turning her face in the direction of the windows*). With the lady whose chimneys we have the honour of contemplating from our windows? (*She moves over up* L.C.)

AUBREY. With Mrs. Cortelyon—yes.

PAULA. Mrs. Cortelyon! The woman who might have set the example of calling on me when we first threw out roots in this deadly-lively soil! Deuce take Mrs. Cortelyon! (*She comes down.*)

AUBREY. Hush! my dear girl!

PAULA (*returning to her seat*). Oh, I know she's an old acquaintance of yours—and of the first Mrs. Tanqueray. And she joins the rest of 'em in slapping the second Mrs. Tanqueray in the face. However, I have my revenge—she's six-and-forty, and I wish nothing worse to happen to any woman.

AUBREY. Well, she's going to town, Cayley says here, and his visit's at an end. He's coming over this morning to call on you. Shall we ask him to transfer himself to us? Do say yes.

PAULA. Yes.

AUBREY (*gladly*). Ah, ha! old Cayley!

PAULA (*coldly*). He'll amuse *you*.

AUBREY. And you too.

PAULA. Because *you* find a companion, shall I be boisterously hilarious?

AUBREY. Come, come! He talks London, and you know you like that.

PAULA. London! (*Putting her chair back.*) London or Heaven! which is farther from me!

AUBREY. Paula!

PAULA. Oh! Oh, I am so bored, Aubrey! (*She leans back wearily.*)

AUBREY (*rising, gathering up his letters, looking at her puzzled and going to her, leaning over her shoulder*). Baby, what can I do for you?

PAULA. I suppose, nothing. You have done all you can for me.

AUBREY. What do you mean?

PAULA. You have married me.

(*He walks away from her thoughtfully, to the writing-table. As he places his letters on the table he sees an addressed letter, stamped for the post, lying on the blotting-book; he picks it up.*)

AUBREY (*in an altered tone*). You've been writing this morning before breakfast?

PAULA (*looking at him quickly, then away again*). Er—that letter.

AUBREY (*coming towards her with the letter in his hand*). To Lady Orreyed. Why?

PAULA. Why not ? Mabel's an old friend of mine.

AUBREY (C.). Are you—corresponding ?

PAULA. I heard from her yesterday. They've just returned from the Riviera. She seems happy.

AUBREY (*sarcastically*). That's good news.

PAULA. Why are you always so cutting about Mabel ? She's a kind-hearted girl. Everything's altered ; she even thinks of letting her hair go back to brown. She's Lady Orreyed. She's married to George. What's the matter with her ?

AUBREY (*turning away*). Oh ! (*He crosses to his seat again.*)

PAULA (*excitedly*). You drive me mad sometimes with the tone you take about things ! (*Jumping up.*) Great goodness, if you come to that, George Orreyed's wife isn't a bit worse than yours ! (*She crosses to* C.)

(*He faces her suddenly.*)

(*Soberly.*) I suppose I needn't have made that observation.

AUBREY. No, there was scarcely a necessity.

(*He throws the letter on to the table* L.C., *and takes up the newspaper and sits* L.C.)

PAULA. I am very sorry. (*Advancing a step or two.*)

AUBREY. All right, dear. (*With a nod, quietly.*)

PAULA (R. *of* L.C. *table, trifling with the letter*). I—I'd better tell you what I've written. I meant to do so, of course. I—I've asked the Orreyeds to come and stay with us.

(*He looks at her and lets the paper fall to the ground in a helpless way.*)

George was a great friend of Cayley's. (*With rising anger.*) I'm sure *he* would be delighted to meet them here.

AUBREY (*throwing his head back, laughing mirthlessly*). Ha, ha, ha ! They say Orreyed has taken to tippling at dinner. Heavens above !

PAULA (*walking away, throws letter down*). Oh ! I've no patience with you ! You'll kill me with this life ! (*She crosses to back of* R. *chair, selects some flowers from a vase on the table*, R.C., *cuts and arranges them, and fastens them in her bodice.*) What is my existence Sunday to Saturday ? In the morning, a drive down to the village with the groom, to give my orders to the tradespeople. At lunch, you and Ellean. (*Playing with nosegay off table.*) In the after-noon, a novel, the newspapers ; if fine, another drive—*if* fine ! Tea—you and Ellean. Then two hours of dusk ; then dinner—you and Ellean. Then a game of Bésique, you and I, while Ellean reads a religious book in a dull corner. Then a yawn from me, another from you, a sigh from Ellean ; three figures suddenly rise—" Good night, good night, good night ! " (*Imitating a kiss.*) " God bless you ! " (*With an exaggerated sigh of dejection and putting nosegay in belt.*) Ah !

AUBREY.   Yes, yes, Paula—yes, dearest—that's what it is *now*.
But, by and by, if people begin to come round us——
   PAULA.   Hah !   (*Advancing to him and standing* R. *of the table.*)
That's where we've made the mistake, my friend Aubrey !   (*Pointing
to the window.*)   Do you believe these people will *ever* come round
us ?   Your former crony, Mrs. Cortelyon ?   Or the grim old vicar,
or that wife of his whose huge nose is positively indecent ?   Or
the Ullathornes, or the Gollans, or Lady William Petres ?   I know
better !   And when the young ones gradually take the place of the
old, there will still remain the sacred tradition that the dreadful
person who lives at the top of the hill is never, under any circumstances, to be called upon !   (*She moves* c.)   And so we shall go
on here, year in and year out, until the sap is run out of our lives,
and we're stale and dry and withered from sheer, solitary respect-
ability.   Upon my word, I wonder we didn't see that we should
have been far happier if we'd gone in for the devil-may-care, *café*-
living sort of life in town !   After all, *I* have a set and you might
have joined it.   It's true I did want, dearly, dearly, to be a married
woman, but where's the pride in being a married woman among
married women who are—married !   If—— (*Seeing that* AUBREY'S
head has sunk into his hands.*)   Aubrey !   My dear boy !   (*She goes
to him.*)   You're not—crying ?

(*He looks up, with a flushed face.*   ELLEAN *enters door up* R.C., *dressed
   very simply for walking.   She is a low-voiced, grave girl of about
   nineteen, with a face somewhat resembling a Madonna.   Towards*
   PAULA *her manner is cold and distant.*)

   AUBREY (*in an undertone*).   Ellean !
   ELLEAN.   Good morning, Papa.   (*Coming down* c.)   Good morning, Paula.

(PAULA *puts her arms round* ELLEAN *and kisses her on the left cheek.*
   ELLEAN *makes little response.*)

   PAULA.   Good morning.   (*Going to the piano—brightly.*)   We've
been breakfasting this side of the house, to get the sun.

(*She sits at the piano and rattles at a gay melody.   Seeing that* PAULA'S
   back is turned to them, ELLEAN *goes to* AUBREY *and kisses him ;
   he returns the kiss almost furtively.   As they separate, the servants
   re-enter door up* R.C.   *The manservant places the chair on which*
   PAULA *has been sitting* R. *of* L.C. *table.   Then both servants proceed
   to carry out the breakfast-table.*)

   AUBREY (*to* ELLEAN *while this is going on*).   I guess where you've
been : there's some gorse clinging to your frock.
   ELLEAN (*removing a sprig of gorse from her skirt*).   Rover and
I walked nearly as far as Black Moor.   The poor fellow has a thorn
in his pad ; I am going upstairs for my tweezers.

AUBREY. Ellean! (*She returns to him.*) Paula is a little depressed—out of sorts. She complains that she has no companion.

ELLEAN. I am with Paula nearly all the day, Papa.

AUBREY. Ah, but you're such a little mouse. Paula likes cheerful people about her.

ELLEAN. I'm afraid I am naturally rather silent; and it's so difficult to seem to be what one is not.

AUBREY. I don't wish that, Ellean.

ELLEAN. I will offer to go down to the village with Paula this morning—shall I ?

AUBREY (*touching her hand gently*). Thank you—do.

ELLEAN. When I've looked after Rover, I'll come back to her.

(*She goes out door down* L. ; PAULA *ceases playing, and turns on the music-stool looking at* AUBREY.)

PAULA. Well, have you and Ellean had your little confidence ? (*She comes down to settee* R.C. *and sits.*)

AUBREY. Confidence ?

PAULA. Do you think I couldn't feel it, like a pain between my shoulders ?

AUBREY (*going to her*). Ellean is coming back in a few minutes to be with you. (*Bending over her.*) Paula, Paula dear, is this how you keep your promise ?

PAULA. Oh ! (*Rising impatiently and crossing swiftly to the settee* L.C., *where he sits, moving restlessly.*) I *can't* keep my promise ; I *am* jealous; it won't be smothered. (*Vehemently.*) I see you looking at her, watching her; your voice drops when you speak to her. I know how fond you are of that girl, Aubrey.

AUBREY. What would you have ? I've no other home for her. She is my daughter.

PAULA. She is your saint. Saint Ellean !

AUBREY (R.C.). You have often told me how good and sweet you think her.

PAULA (C.). Good !—yes. Do you imagine *that* makes me less jealous ? (*Going to him and clinging to his arm.*) Aubrey, there are two sorts of affection—the love for a woman you respect, and the love for a woman you—love. She gets the first from you : I never can.

AUBREY. Hush, hush ! you don't realize what you say.

PAULA. If Ellean cared for me only a little, it would be different. I shouldn't be jealous then. Why doesn't she care for me ?

AUBREY. She—she—she will, in time.

PAULA. You can't say that without stuttering.

AUBREY. Her disposition seems a little unresponsive ; she resembles her mother in many ways ; I can see it every day.

PAULA. She's marble. It's a shame. There's not the slightest excuse ; for all she knows, I'm as much a saint as she—only married. Dearest, help me to win her over !

AUBREY. Help you ?

PAULA. You can. (*Persuasively.*) Teach her that it is her duty to love me; she hangs on to every word you speak. I'm sure, Aubrey, that the love of a nice woman who believed me to be like herself would do me a world of good. You'd get the benefit of it as well as I. It would soothe me; it would make me less horribly restless; it would take this—this—mischievous feeling from me. (*Coaxingly.*) Aubrey!

AUBREY. Have patience; everything will come right.

PAULA. Yes, if you help me.

AUBREY. In the meantime you will tear up your letter to Lady Orreyed, won't you?

PAULA (*kissing his hand*). Of course I will—anything! (*She moves away from him to* L.C. *table and standing at back of it picks up letter.*)

AUBREY. Ah, thank you, dearest! (*Laughing.*) Just imagine " Saint Ellean " and that woman side by side! (*He crosses* R. *to fire.*)

PAULA (*going back with a cry*). Ah!

AUBREY. What?

PAULA (*passionately*). It's Ellean you're considering, not me! It's all Ellean with you! Ellean! Ellean!

(ELLEAN *re-enters, door down* L.)

ELLEAN. Did you call me, Paula?

(*Clenching his hands,* AUBREY *turns away and goes out door up* R.C.) Is Papa angry?

PAULA (*shrugging her shoulders*). I drive him distracted sometimes. (*Walking away to settee* R. *and sitting, petulantly.*) There, I confess it!

ELLEAN (*advancing*). Do you? Oh, why do you?

PAULA. Because I—because I'm jealous.

ELLEAN (*jealous*). Jealous?

PAULA. Yes—of you.

(ELLEAN *is silent.*)

(*Facing her.*) Well, what do you think of that?

ELLEAN. I knew it; I've seen it. It hurts me dreadfully. What do you wish me to do? (*By chair* L.C.) Go away?

PAULA. Leave us! (*Beckoning her with a motion of the head.*) Look here!

(ELLEAN *goes to* PAULA *slowly and unresponsively.*)

You could cure me of my jealousy very easily. Why don't you— like me?

ELLEAN (*tremblingly*). What do you mean by—like you? I don't understand.

PAULA. Love me.

ELLEAN. Love is not a feeling that is under one's control. I shall alter as time goes on, perhaps. (*She moves* c.) I didn't begin to love my father deeply till a few months ago, and then I obeyed my mother.

PAULA (*dryly*). Ah, yes, you dream things, don't you—see them in your sleep? You fancy your mother speaks to you?

ELLEAN. When you have lost your mother it is a comfort to believe that she is dead only to this life, that she still watches over her child. I do believe that of my mother.

PAULA (*slowly*). Well, and so you haven't been bidden to love *me*?

ELLEAN (*after a pause, almost inaudibly*). No. (*Moves to chair.*)

PAULA. Dreams are only a hash-up of one's day-thoughts, I suppose you know. Think intently of anything, and it's bound to come back to you at night. I don't cultivate dreams myself.

ELLEAN. Ah, I knew you would only sneer! (*She sits* L.C.)

PAULA. I'm not sneering; I'm speaking the truth. (*Rising.*) I say that if you cared for me in the daytime I should soon make friends with those nightmares of yours. (*Eyeing her askance, hesitatingly.*) Ellean, why don't you try to look on me as your second mother?

(ELLEAN *gives* PAULA *a quick look, then sits motionless.*)

Of course there are not many years between us, but I'm ever so much older than you—in experience. I shall have no children of my own, I know that; it would be a real comfort to me if you would make me feel we belonged to each other. Won't you?

(ELLEAN *rises and stands front of* L.C. *table.*)

Perhaps you think I'm odd—not nice. Well, the fact is I've two sides to my nature, and I've let the one almost smother the other. A few years ago I went through some trouble, and since then I haven't shed a tear. I believe if you put your arms round me just once I should run upstairs and have a good cry. There, I've talked to you as I've never talked to a woman in my life. Ellean, you seem to fear me. Don't! Kiss me!

(*With a cry, almost of despair,* ELLEAN *turns from* PAULA, *and sinks on to the settee* L., *covering her face with her hands.*)

(*Indignantly.*) Oh! Why is it! How dare you treat me like this? What do you mean by it? What do you mean?

(*A* SERVANT *enters.*)

SERVANT. Mr. Drummle, ma'am.

(CAYLEY DRUMMLE, *in riding dress, enters briskly and comes down to* PAULA. *The* SERVANT *retires.*)

PAULA (*recovering herself*). Well, Cayley! (*She crosses to the fireplace.*)

DRUMMLE (*shaking hands with her cordially*). How are you?

(*Shaking hands with* ELLEAN, *who rises.*) I saw you in the distance an hour ago, in the gorse near Stapleton's.

ELLEAN. I didn't see you, Mr. Drummle.

DRUMMLE. My dear Ellean, it is my experience that no charming young lady of nineteen ever does see a man of forty-five. (*Laughing.*) Ha, ha !

ELLEAN (*crossing in front of him and going to the door*). Paula, Papa wishes me to drive down to the village with you this morning. Do you care to take me ?

PAULA (*coldly*). Oh, by all means. Pray tell Watts to balance the cart for three.

(ELLEAN *goes out.*)

DRUMMLE (*crossing* R.C.). How's Aubrey ?

PAULA. Very well—when Ellean's about the house.

DRUMMLE. And you ? I needn't ask.

PAULA (*walking away to the window*). Oh, a dog's life, my dear Cayley, mine.

DRUMMLE (*crossing* R.C., *turning, watching her*). Eh ?

PAULA. Doesn't that define a happy marriage ? I'm sleek, well-kept, well-fed, never without a bone to gnaw and fresh straw to lie upon. (*Gazing out of the window.*) Oh, dear me !

DRUMMLE (*to himself*). H'm. (*Crossing to the fireplace—aloud.*) Well, I heartily congratulate you on your kennel. The view from the terrace here is superb.

PAULA. Yes, I can see London.

DRUMMLE. London ! Not quite so far, surely ?

PAULA. *I* can. (*Turning.*) Also the Mediterranean, on a fine day. I wonder what Algiers looks like this morning from the sea ! (*Coming down impulsively.*) Oh, Cayley, do you remember those jolly times on board Peter Jarman's yacht when we lay off—— ? (*Stopping suddenly, seeing* DRUMMLE *staring at her—half to herself.*) Good gracious ! What are we talking about ! (*She moves* L.C.)

(AUBREY *enters, door up* R.C., *which he leaves open.*)

AUBREY (*coming down to* DRUMMLE). Dear old chap ! Has Paula asked you ?

PAULA. Not yet.

AUBREY. We want you to come to us, now that you're leaving Mrs. Cortelyon—at once, to-day. Stay a month, as long as you please—eh, Paula ?

PAULA. As long as you can possibly endure it—do, Cayley.

DRUMMLE (*looking at* AUBREY). Delighted. (*Advancing to* PAULA.) Charming of you to have me.

PAULA. My dear man, you're a blessing. Ha ! Ha ! I must telegraph to London for more fish ! A strange appetite to cater for ! (*Almost childishly delighted.*) Something to do, to do, to do !

(*She goes out door, down* L.)

DRUMMLE (L.C., *eyeing* AUBREY). Well?

AUBREY (*with a wearied, anxious look*). Well, Cayley?

DRUMMLE. How are you getting on?

AUBREY. My position doesn't grow less difficult. (*He goes up stage and shuts door; then comes down* R.C. *and sits.*) I told you, when I met you last week, of this feverish, jealous attachment of Paula's for Ellean?

DRUMMLE. Yes. I hardly know why, but I came to the conclusion that you don't consider it an altogether fortunate attachment.

AUBREY (*troubled*). Ellean doesn't respond to it.

DRUMMLE. These are early days. Ellean will warm towards your wife by and by. (*Soothingly.*)

AUBREY (*striking the arm of the settee nervously*). Ah, but there's the question, Cayley!

DRUMMLE. What question?

AUBREY. The question which positively distracts me. Ellean is so different from—most women; I don't believe a purer creature exists out of heaven. (*With difficulty.*) And I—I ask myself, am I doing right in exposing her to the influence of poor Paula's light, careless nature?

DRUMMLE (*in a low voice*). My dear Aubrey! (*He moves* L.C.)

AUBREY. That shocks you! So it does me. (*Rising.*) I assure you I long to urge my girl to break down the reserve which keeps her apart from Paula, but somehow I can't do it—well, I don't do it.

(DRUMMLE *sits* L.C.)

How can I make you understand? But when you come to us you'll understand quickly enough. Cayley, there's hardly a subject you can broach on which poor Paula hasn't some strange, out-of-the-way thought to give utterance to; some curious, warped notion. They are not mere worldly thoughts—unless, good God! they belong to the little hellish world which our blackguardism has created: no, her ideas have too little calculation in them to be called worldly. But it makes it the more dreadful that such thoughts should be ready, spontaneous; that expressing them has become a perfectly natural process; that her words, acts even, have almost lost their proper significance for her, and seem beyond her control. (*Going to him.*) Ah, and the pain of listening to it all from the woman one loves, the woman one hoped to make happy and contented, who is really and truly a good woman, as it were, maimed! Well, this is my burden, and I shouldn't speak to you of it but for my anxiety about Ellean. Ellean! What is to be her future? It is in my hands; what am I to do? Cayley, when I remember how Ellean comes to me, from another world I always think, when I realize the charge that's laid on me, I find myself wishing, in a sort of terror, that my child were safe under the ground!

(*He walks away up to the writing-table and sits apart.* DRUMMLE *crosses to the fire thoughtfully.*)

DRUMMLE (R.). My dear Aubrey, aren't you making a mistake ?

AUBREY (*not turning*). Very likely. What is it ?

DRUMMLE. A mistake, not in regarding your Ellean as an angel, but in believing that under any circumstances, it would be possible for her to go through life without getting her white robe—shall we say, a little dusty at the hem ? (*He moves to top end of settee R.C. and sits.*) Don't take me for a cynic. I am sure there are many women upon earth who are almost divinely innocent ; but being on earth, they must send their robes to the laundry occasionally. Ah, and it's right that they should have to do so, for what can they learn from the checking of their little washing-bills but lessons of charity ? Now I see but two courses open to you for the disposal of your angel.

AUBREY. Yes ?

DRUMMLE (*looking round at room*). You must either restrict her to a paradise which is, like every earthly paradise, necessarily somewhat imperfect, or treat her as an ordinary flesh-and-blood young woman, and give her the advantages of that society to which she properly belongs.

AUBREY (*turning to* DRUMMLE). Advantages ?

DRUMMLE. My dear Aubrey, of all forms of innocence mere ignorance is the least admirable. Take my advice, let her walk and talk and suffer and be healed with the great crowd. Do it, and hope that she'll some day meet a good, honest fellow who'll make her life complete, happy, secure. Now you see what I'm driving at.

AUBREY. A sanguine programme, my dear Cayley ! (*Rising and coming down.*) Oh, I'm not pooh-poohing it. Putting sentiment aside, of course I know that a fortunate marriage for Ellean would be the best—perhaps the only—solution of my difficulty. But you forget the danger of the course you suggest.

DRUMMLE. Danger ?

AUBREY. If Ellean goes among men and women, how can she escape from learning, sooner or later, the history of—poor Paula's —old life ?

DRUMMLE. H'm ! (*He rises.*) You remember the episode of the Jeweller's Son in the Arabian Nights ? Of course you don't. (*Earnestly.*) Well, if your daughter lives, she *can't* escape—what you're afraid of.

(AUBREY *gives a half-stifled exclamation of pain, leaves* DRUMMLE *and sits.*)

(*Going to him.*) And when she does hear the story, surely it would be better that she should have some knowledge of the world to help her to understand it.

AUBREY. To understand !

DRUMMLE. To understand, to—to philosophize.

AUBREY. To philosophize ?

DRUMMLE.   Philosophy is toleration, and it is only one step from toleration to forgiveness.

AUBREY.   You're right, Cayley ; I believe you always are.   Yes, yes.   But, even if I had the courage to attempt to solve the problem of Ellean's future in this way, I—I'm helpless.

DRUMMLE.   How ?

AUBREY.   What means have I now of placing my daughter in the world I've left ?

DRUMMLE.   Oh, some friend—some woman friend.

AUBREY (*in a low voice*).   I have none ; they're gone.

DRUMMLE.   You're wrong there ; I know one——

AUBREY (*rising—listening*).   That's Paula's cart.   (*Walking across to the fireplace.*)   Let's discuss this again.

DRUMMLE (*going up to the window and looking out*).   It isn't the dog-cart.   (*Turning to* AUBREY.)   I hope you'll forgive me, old chap.

AUBREY.   What for ?

DRUMMLE.   Whose wheels do you think have been cutting ruts in your immaculate drive ?

(*A* SERVANT *enters, door up* R.O.)

SERVANT (*to* AUBREY).   Mrs. Cortelyon, sir.

AUBREY.   Mrs. Cortelyon !   (*After a short pause.*)   Very well.

(*The* SERVANT *withdraws.*)

What on earth is the meaning of this ?

DRUMMLE (*coming down* C.).   Ahem !   While I've been our old friend's guest, Aubrey, we have very naturally talked a good deal about you and yours.

AUBREY (*dryly*).   Indeed, have you ?

DRUMMLE.   Yes, and Alice Cortelyon has arrived at the conclusion that it would have been far kinder had she called on Mrs. Tanqueray long ago.   (*Slyly.*)   She's going abroad for Easter before settling down in London for the season, and I believe she has come over this morning to ask for Ellean's companionship.

AUBREY.   Oh, I see !   (*Frowning.*)   Quite a friendly little conspiracy, my dear Cayley !

DRUMMLE.   Conspiracy !   Not at all, I assure you.   (*Laughing.*)   Ha, ha !

(ELLEAN *enters from the hall door up* R.O., *with* MRS. CORTELYON, *a handsome, good-humoured, spirited woman of about forty-five.*)

ELLEAN (*up* C.).   Papa——

(DRUMMLE *joins* ELLEAN *and stands talking when in doorway.*)

MRS. CORTELYON (*coming down to* AUBREY, *and shaking hands with him heartily*).   Well, Aubrey, how are you ?   I've just been telling this great girl of yours that I knew her when she was a sad-

faced, pale baby. How is Mrs. Tanqueray? I have been a bad
neighbour, and I'm here to beg forgiveness. Is she indoors?

AUBREY. She's upstairs putting on a hat, I believe.

MRS. CORTELYON (*sitting* c., *comfortably*). Ah! (*She looks
round.*) We used to be very frank with each other, Aubrey. I
suppose the old footing is no longer possible, eh?

AUBREY. If so, I'm not entirely to blame, Mrs. Cortelyon.

MRS. CORTELYON. Mrs. Cortelyon? H'm! No, I admit it.
But you must make some little allowance for me, *Mr. Tanqueray.*
Your first wife and I, as girls, were like two cherries on one stalk,
and then I was the confidential friend of your married life. That
post, perhaps, wasn't altogether a sinecure. And now—well, when
a woman gets to my age I suppose she's a stupid, prejudiced, conventional creature. However, I've got over it and—(*giving him her
hand*)—I hope you'll be enormously happy and let me be a friend
once more.

AUBREY. Thank you, Alice.

MRS. CORTELYON. That's right. I feel more cheerful than I've
done for weeks. But I suppose it would serve me right if the second
Mrs. Tanqueray showed me the door. Do you think she will?

AUBREY (*listening*). Here is my wife.

(MRS. CORTELYON *rises and moves* C. *and* PAULA *enters, door down*
L., *dressed for driving ; she stops abruptly on seeing* MRS. CORTELYON.
ELLEAN *slowly moves to window and sits.* DRUMMLE *remains
standing in doorway. He afterwards moves down* R. *to fireplace.*)

(R.C.) Paula dear, Mrs. Cortelyon has called to see you.

(PAULA *starts, looks at* MRS. CORTELYON *irresolutely, then after a
slight pause barely touches* MRS. CORTELYON'S *extended hand.*)

PAULA (*whose manner now alternates between deliberate insolence
and assumed sweetness*). Mrs.——? What name, Aubrey?

AUBREY. Mrs. Cortelyon.

PAULA. Cortelyon? Oh, yes. Cortelyon.

MRS. CORTELYON (*carefully guarding herself throughout against any
expression of resentment*). Aubrey ought to have told you that
Alice Cortelyon and he are very old friends.

PAULA. Oh, very likely he has mentioned the circumstance. I
have quite a wretched memory.

MRS. CORTELYON. You know we are neighbours, Mrs. Tanqueray.

PAULA. Neighbours? Are we really? Won't you sit down?

(*They both sit.* MRS. CORTELYON *sits* R.C., PAULA C.)

Neighbours! That's most interesting!

MRS. CORTELYON. Very near neighbours. You can see my roof
from your windows.

PAULA. I fancy I *have* observed a roof. But you have been
away from home ; you have only just returned.

Mrs. Cortelyon. I ? What makes you think that ?

Paula. Why, because it is two months since we came to Higher-coombe, and I don't remember your having called.

Mrs. Cortelyon. Your memory is now terribly accurate. No, I've not been away from home, and it is to explain my neglect that I am here, rather unceremoniously, this morning.

Paula. Oh, to explain—quite so. (*With mock solicitude. She rises and goes to her.*) Ah, you've been very ill ; I ought to have seen that before.

Mrs. Cortelyon. Ill !

Paula. You look dreadfully pulled down. We poor women show illness so plainly in our faces, don't we ?

Aubrey (*behind table* l.c.—*anxiously*). Paula dear, Mrs. Cortelyon is the picture of health.

Mrs. Cortelyon (*with some asperity*). I have never *felt* better in my life.

Paula (*looking round innocently*). Have I said anything awkward ? (*Turning to* Aubrey.) Aubrey, tell Mrs. Cortelyon how stupid and thoughtless I always am ! (*She sits* l.c.)

(Drummle, *who has been watching the two ladies, is now on* Mrs. Cortelyon's r.)

Mrs. Cortelyon (*aside to* Drummle, *who is now standing close to her*). Really, Cayley——

(*He soothes her with a nod and smile and a motion of his finger to his lip, then wanders away again up* r.)

Mrs. Tanqueray, I am afraid my explanation will not be quite so satisfactory as either of those you have just helped me to. You may have heard—but, if you have heard, you have doubtless forgotten—that twenty years ago, when your husband first lived here, I was a constant visitor at Highercoombe.

Paula. Twenty years ago—fancy ! I was a naughty little child then.

Mrs. Cortelyon. Possibly. Well, at that time, and till the end of her life, my affections were centred upon the lady of this house.

Paula. Were they ? That was very sweet of you.

(Ellean *creeps down quietly to* Mrs. Cortelyon, *listening intently to her.*)

Mrs. Cortelyon. I will say no more on that score, but I must add this : when, two months ago, you came here, I realized, perhaps for the first time, that I was a middle-aged woman, and that it had become impossible for me to accept without some effort a breaking-in upon many tender associations. There, Mrs. Tanqueray, that is my confession. Will you try to understand it and pardon me ?

Paula (*watching* Ellean—*sneeringly*). Ellean dear, you appear to be very interested in Mrs. Cortelyon's reminiscences ; I don't think I can do better than make you my mouthpiece—there is such sympathy between us. (*Leaning back languidly.*) What do you say—can we bring ourselves to forgive Mrs. Cortelyon for neglecting us for two weary months ?

MRS. CORTELYON (*to* ELLEAN, *pleasantly*). Well, Ellean ? (*With a little cry of tenderness* ELLEAN *impulsively sits beside* MRS. CORTELYON *and takes her hand.*) My dear child ! (ELLEAN *sits with* MRS. CORTELYON *on settee* R.)

PAULA (*in an undertone to* AUBREY). Ellean isn't so very slow in taking to Mrs. Cortelyon !

MRS. CORTELYON (*to* PAULA *and* AUBREY). Come, this encourages me to broach my scheme. Mrs. Tanqueray, it strikes me that you two good people are just now excellent company for each other, while Ellean would perhaps be glad of a little peep into the world you are anxious to avoid. Now, I'm going to Paris to-morrow for a week or two before settling down in Chester Square, so—don't gasp, both of you !—if this girl is willing, and you have made no other arrangements for her, will you let her come with me to Paris, and afterwards remain with me in town during the Season ?

(ELLEAN *utters an exclamation of surprise.* PAULA *is silent.*)

(*After a pause.*) What do you say ?

AUBREY (L.C., *gently*). Paula—Paula dear. (*Hesitatingly, moves* C.) My dear Mrs. Cortelyon, this is wonderfully kind of you ; I am really at a loss to—eh, Cayley ?

DRUMMLE (*up stage, watching* PAULA *apprehensively*). Kind ! Now I must say I don't think so ! I begged Alice to take *me* to Paris, and she declined. I am thrown over for Ellean ! Ha ! ha !

MRS. CORTELYON (*laughing*). What nonsense you talk, Cayley !

(*The laughter dies out.* PAULA *remains quite still.*)

AUBREY. Paula dear. (*He crosses to* PAULA'S *chair and stands behind table.*)

PAULA (*slowly collecting herself*). One moment. I—I don't quite—— (*To* MRS. CORTELYON.) You propose that Ellean leaves Highercoombe almost at once and remains with you some months ?

MRS. CORTELYON. It would be a mercy to me. You can afford to be generous to a desolate old widow. Come, Mrs. Tanqueray, won't you spare her ?

PAULA. Won't *I* spare her. (*Suspiciously.*) Have you mentioned your plan to Aubrey—before I came in ?

MRS. CORTELYON. No, I had no opportunity.

PAULA. Nor to Ellean ?

MRS. CORTELYON. Oh, no.

PAULA (*looking about her, in suppressed excitement*). This hasn't been discussed at all, behind my back ?

MRS. CORTELYON. My dear Mrs. Tanqueray !

PAULA (*forcing her chair back a little*). Ellean, let us hear your voice in the matter!

ELLEAN. I should like to go with Mrs. Cortelyon——

PAULA. Ah!

ELLEAN. That is, if—if——

PAULA. If—if what?

ELLEAN (*looking towards* AUBREY, *appealingly*). Papa?

PAULA (*in a hard voice*). Oh, of course—I forgot. (*To* AUBREY.) My dear Aubrey, it rests with you, naturally, whether I am—to lose —Ellean.

AUBREY (*brightly*). Lose Ellean! (*Advancing to* PAULA.) There is no question of losing Ellean. (*Going to* C.) You would see Ellean in town constantly when she returned from Paris; isn't that so, Mrs. Cortelyon? (*Crosses more* C.R.)

MRS. CORTELYON. Certainly.

PAULA (*laughing softly*). Oh, I didn't know I should be allowed that privilege.

MRS. CORTELYON. Privilege, my dear Mrs. Tanqueray!

PAULA. Ha, ha! that makes all the difference, doesn't it?

AUBREY (*with assumed gaiety*). All the difference? I should think so! (*To* ELLEAN, *laying his hand upon her head, tenderly.*) And you are quite certain you wish to see what the world is like on the other side of Black Moor?

ELLEAN (*in a low voice*). If you are willing, Papa, I am quite certain. (*She rises.*)

AUBREY (*looking at* PAULA *irresolutely, then speaking with an effort*). Then I—I am willing.

PAULA (*rising and striking the table lightly with her clenched hand*). That decides it!

(*There is a general movement.* AUBREY *and* ELLEAN *go up stage;* MRS. CORTELYON *advances to* PAULA, DRUMMLE *remains in front of fire.*)

(*Excitedly to* MRS. CORTELYON, *who advances towards her.*) When do you want her?

MRS. CORTELYON. We go to town this afternoon at five o'clock, and sleep to-night at Bayliss's. There is barely time for her to make her preparations.

PAULA. I will undertake that she is ready.

MRS. CORTELYON. I've a great deal to scramble through at home too, as you may guess. Good-bye! (*She offers her hand.*)

PAULA (*turning away*). Mrs. Cortelyon is going.

(PAULA *stands up* L.C., *looking out of the window, with her back to those in the room.* DRUMMLE *comes down to* MRS. CORTELYON.)

MRS. CORTELYON (*aside to* DRUMMLE). Cayley——

DRUMMLE (*aside to her*). Eh?

MRS. CORTELYON. I've gone through it, for the sake of Aubrey and his child, but I—I feel a hundred. Is that a mad-woman?

DRUMMLE. Of course; all jealous women are mad.

(*He goes up and exits* R. *with* AUBREY. MRS. CORTELYON *moves up stage* C.)

MRS. CORTELYON (*hesitatingly, to* PAULA). Good-bye, Mrs. Tanqueray.

(PAULA *inclines her head with the slightest possible movement, then resumes her former position.* ELLEAN *comes from the hall and takes* MRS. CORTELYON *out of the room off* R. *After a brief silence,* PAULA *turns with a fierce cry, and hurriedly takes off her coat and hat, almost tearing them from her, and tosses them upon the settee,* L.C. *Upon removing her hat, she stabs it viciously with long fastener.*)

PAULA. Oh! Oh! Oh!

(*She drops into the chair* C. *as* AUBREY *returns; he stands up* R.C., *looking at her.*)

Who's that?

AUBREY (*coming down*). I. You have altered your mind about going out?

PAULA. Yes. Please to ring the bell.

AUBREY (*touching the bell on wall* R.). You are angry about Mrs. Cortelyon and Ellean. Let me try to explain my reasons—— (*He returns* C.)

PAULA. Be careful what you say to me just now! I have never felt like this—except once—in my life. (*With great intensity.*) Be careful what you say to me!

(*A* SERVANT *enters, door* R.C.)

(*Rising.*) Is Watts at the door with the cart?

SERVANT (*coming down*). Yes, ma'am.

PAULA (*picking up the letter which has been lying upon the table,* L.C.). Tell him to drive down to the post office directly, with this.

AUBREY (*advancing a step*). With that?

PAULA (*calmly*). Yes. My letter to Lady Orreyed.

(*She gives the letter to the* SERVANT, *who goes out.*)

AUBREY (*quickly*). Surely you don't wish me to countermand any order of yours to a servant? Call the man back—take the letter from him!

PAULA. I have not the slightest intention of doing so.

AUBREY (*going to the door* R.C.). I must, then.

(*She snatches up her hat and coat and follows him.*)

What are you going to do?

PAULA. If you stop that letter, walk out of the house.

(*He hesitates, then leaves the door, and comes down* R.C.)

Aubrey. I am right in believing that to be the letter inviting George Orreyed and his wife to stay here, am I not ?

Paula. Oh yes—quite right.

Aubrey. Let it go ; I'll write to him by and by.

Paula (*coming down to him and facing him*). You dare !

Aubrey (*pained at her violence*). Hush, Paula !

Paula. Insult me again and, upon my word, I'll go straight out of the house !

Aubrey. Insult you ?

Paula. Insult me ! What else is it ? My God ! what else is it ? (*Throwing her hat and coat on table* c.) What do you mean by taking Ellean from me ? (*She goes* c.)

Aubrey. Listen——!

Paula. Listen to *me* ! (*Volubly.*) And how do you take her ? You pack her off in the care of a woman who has deliberately held aloof from me, who's thrown mud at me ! Yet this Cortelyon creature has only to put foot here once to be entrusted with the charge of the girl you know I dearly want to keep near me ! (*She moves* L.C.)

Aubrey (*entreatingly*). Paula dear ! hear me——!

Paula. Ah ! of course, of course ! (*She here speaks with passionate volubility and self-conviction.*) I can't be so useful to your daughter as such people as this ; and so I'm to be given the go-by for any town friend of yours who turns up and chooses to patronize us ! Hah ! Very well, at any rate, as you take Ellean from me you justify my looking for companions where I can most readily find 'em. (*She goes to back of table.*)

Aubrey. You wish me to fully appreciate your reason for sending that letter to Lady Orreyed ?

Paula (*taking up her hat and coat*). Precisely—I do.

Aubrey (*facing her*). And could you, after all, go back to associates of that order ? It's not possible !

Paula (*mockingly*). What, not after the refining influence of these intensely respectable surroundings ? (*Going to the door down* L.) We'll see !

Aubrey. Paula !

Paula (*violently*). We'll see !

(*She goes out. He stands still looking after her.*)

The Curtain *falls.*

ACT III

SCENE.—*The drawing-room at "Highercoombe." The scene is set obliquely and runs up the stage from* R. *to* L. *In the wall at back are a door opening into a small hall and two large French windows, sheltered by a verandah, leading into the garden. The door is* R., *the windows* R.C. *and* L.C. *In the wall on the* L. *are double doors, recessed, and a fireplace, the former up stage, the latter down stage. The fireplace is decorated with flowers; over the fireplace a large mirror; before the fireplace, a settee.* L.C., *a table. Above table, a chair; below table, a footstool. On the* R. *of table, an armchair. On the table, knick-knacks in silver—small hand-mirror, etc., also a book or two. Up* C., *between the windows, a settee.* R.C., *by the window, an armchair.* R.C., *down stage, a circular ottoman.* R., *a grand pianoforte, open, and music-stool. Music on or by the piano. Other articles of furniture to fill spaces. Flowers, lamps, etc. Everything costly and tasteful. The windows are open at the beginning of the act. Moonlight in the garden.*

LADY ORREYED, *a pretty, affected doll of a woman with a mincing voice and flaxen hair, is sitting on the ottoman* R.C., *her head resting against the drum, and her eyes closed.* PAULA, *looking pale, worn, and thoroughly unhappy, is sitting at a table* L.C. *Both are in sumptuous dinner-gowns.*

LADY ORREYED (*opening her eyes*). Well, I never! I dropped off! (*Feeling her hair.*) Just fancy! Where are the men?
PAULA (*icily*). Outside, smoking.

(*A* SERVANT *enters door* R. *with coffee, which he hands to* LADY OR-REYED. SIR GEORGE ORREYED *comes in by the window* L.C. *He is a man of about thirty-five, with a low forehead, a receding chin, a vacuous expression, and an ominous redness about the nose.*)

LADY ORREYED (*taking coffee*). Here's Dodo.
SIR GEORGE. I say, the flies under the verandah make you swear. (*He moves down* R.C.)

(*The* SERVANT *hands coffee to* PAULA, *who declines it, then to* SIR GEORGE, *who takes a cup. The* SERVANT *goes up* L.)

Hi! wait a bit! (*He looks at the tray searchingly, then puts back his cup.*) Never mind.

(*The* SERVANT *moves away.*)

(*Quietly to* LADY ORREYED.) I say, they're dooced sparin' with their liqueur, ain't they?

40

(*The* SERVANT *goes out at window* R.C. *and off up* L.)

PAULA (*to* SIR GEORGE). Won't you take coffee, George?

(LADY ORREYED *puts her coffee-cup on the piano.*)

SIR GEORGE (*pulling his moustache*). No, thanks. It's gettin' near time for a whisky and potass. (*Approaching* PAULA, *regarding* LADY ORREYED *admiringly.*) I say, Birdie looks rippin' to-night, don't she?

PAULA. Your wife?

SIR GEORGE. Yaas—Birdie.

PAULA. Rippin'?

SIR GEORGE. Yaas.

PAULA. Quite—quite rippin'. (*She rises and goes up* R.C.)

(*He moves round to the settee* L. PAULA *watches him with distaste.* SIR GEORGE *falls asleep on the settee by fireplace.* LADY ORREYED *returns to the front seat of the ottoman.*)

LADY ORREYED. Paula love, I fancied you and Aubrey were a little more friendly at dinner. You haven't made it up, have you?

PAULA. We? Oh, no. We speak before others, that's all.

LADY ORREYED. And how long do you intend to carry on this game, dear?

PAULA (*turning away impatiently*). I really can't tell you.

LADY ORREYED. Sit down, old girl; don't be so fidgety.

(PAULA *sits on the upper seat of the ottoman with her back to* LADY ORREYED.)

Of course, it's my duty, as an old friend, to give you a good talking to—

(PAULA *glares at her suddenly and fiercely.*)

—(*unconsciously*) but really I've found one gets so many smacks in the face through interfering in matrimonial squabbles that I've determined to drop it.

PAULA (*emphatically*). I think you're wise.

LADY ORREYED. However, I must say that I do wish you'd look at marriage in a more solemn light—just as I do, in fact. It is such a beautiful thing—marriage, and if people in our position don't respect it, and set a good example by living happily with their husbands, what can you expect from the middle classes? When did this sad state of affairs between you and Aubrey actually begin?

PAULA. Actually, a fortnight and three days ago; I haven't calculated the minutes.

LADY ORREYED. A day or two before Dodo and I turned up—arrived.

PAULA. Yes. One always remembers one thing by another; we left off speaking to each other the morning I wrote asking you to visit us.

LADY ORREYED. Lucky for you I was able to pop down, wasn't it, dear ?

PAULA (*glaring at her again*). Most fortunate.

LADY ORREYED. A serious split with your husband without a pal on the premises—I should say, without a friend in the house—would be most unpleasant.

PAULA (*rising and turning to her abruptly*). This place must be horribly doleful for you and George just now. At least you ought to consider him before me. Why don't you leave me to my difficulties ? (*She sits beside her.*)

LADY ORREYED. Oh, we're quite comfortable, dear, thank you—both of us. George and me are so wrapped up in each other, it doesn't matter where we are. I don't want to crow over you, old girl, but I've got a perfect husband.

(SIR GEORGE *is now fast asleep, his head thrown back and his mouth open, looking hideous.*)

PAULA (*glancing at* SIR GEORGE). So you've given me to understand.

LADY ORREYED. Not that we don't have our little differences. Why, we fell out only this very morning. You remember the diamond and ruby tiara Charley Prestwick gave poor dear Connie Tirlemont years ago, don't you ?

PAULA (*emphatically*). No, I do not.

LADY ORREYED. No ? Well, it's in the market. Benjamin of Piccadilly has got it in his shop-window, and I've set my heart on it.

PAULA. You consider it quite necessary ?

LADY ORREYED. Yes, because what I say to Dodo is this—a lady of my station must smother herself with hair ornaments. It's different with you, love—people don't look for so much blaze from you, but I've got rank to keep up ; haven't I ?

PAULA. Yes.

LADY ORREYED. Well, that was the cause of the little set-to between I and Dodo this morning. He broke two chairs, he was in such a rage. I forgot, they're your chairs ; do you mind ?

PAULA. No.

LADY ORREYED. You know, poor Dodo can't lose his temper without smashing something ; if it isn't a chair, it's a mirror ; if it isn't that, it's china—a bit of Dresden for choice. Dear old pet ! he loves a bit of Dresden when he's furious. He doesn't really throw things *at* me, dear ; he simply lifts them up and drops them, like a gentleman. I expect our room upstairs will look rather wrecky before I get that tiara.

PAULA. Excuse the suggestion, perhaps your husband can't afford it.

LADY ORREYED. Oh, how dreadfully changed you are, Paula ! Dodo can always mortgage something, or borrow of his ma. What *is* coming to you !

PAULA (*rising*). Ah! (*She sits at the piano and touches the keys.*)

LADY ORREYED (*turning to* PAULA). Oh, yes, do play! That's the one thing I envy you for. (*She rises and sits* R. *of the ottoman.*)

PAULA. What shall I play?

LADY ORREYED. What was that heavenly piece you gave us last night, dear?

PAULA. A bit of Schubert. Would you like to hear it again?

LADY ORREYED (*thoughtfully*). You don't know any comic songs, do you?

PAULA. I'm afraid not.

LADY ORREYED (*settling herself*). I leave it to you, then.

(PAULA *plays.* AUBREY *and* CAYLEY DRUMMLE *appear outside the window* L.C. ; *they look into the room.*)

AUBREY (*to* DRUMMLE, *drawing back*). You can see her face in that mirror. Poor girl, how ill and wretched she looks.

DRUMMLE. When are the Orreyeds going?

AUBREY (*entering the room*). Heaven knows!

DRUMMLE (*following* AUBREY). But *you're* entertaining them; what's it to do with Heaven?

AUBREY. Do you know, Cayley, that even the Orreyeds serve a useful purpose? My wife actually speaks to me before our guests —think of that! I've come to rejoice at the presence of the Orreyeds!

DRUMMLE. I daresay; we're taught that beetles are sent for a benign end.

AUBREY. Cayley, talk to Paula again to-night.

DRUMMLE. Certainly, if I get the chance.

AUBREY. Let's contrive it. George is asleep; perhaps I can get that doll out of the way.

(*They go down stage. As they advance into the room,* PAULA *abruptly ceases playing and finds interest in a volume of music.* SIR GEORGE *is now nodding and snoring apoplectically.*)

Lady Orreyed, whenever you feel inclined for a game of billiards I'm at your service.

LADY ORREYED (*jumping up*). Charmed, I'm sure! I really thought you'd forgotten poor little me. Oh, look at Dodo! (*She crosses to him, back of table.*)

AUBREY. No, no, don't wake him; he's tired.

LADY ORREYED. I must, he looks so plain. (*Rousing* SIR GEORGE.) Dodo! Dodo! (*She lightly flicks his face with her fan.*)

SIR GEORGE (*stupidly*). 'Ullo!

LADY ORREYED. Dodo, dear, you were snoring.

SIR GEORGE. Oh, I say, you could 'a told me that by and by.

AUBREY. You want a cigar, George; come into the billiard-room. (*Giving his arm to* LADY ORREYED.) Cayley, bring Paula.

(AUBREY *and* LADY ORREYED *go out door* L.)

SIR GEORGE (*rising and going* C.). Hey, what! Billiard-room! (*Looking at his watch.*) How goes the——? Phew! 'Ullo, 'Ullo! Whisky and Potass!

(*He goes rapidly after* AUBREY *and* LADY ORREYED. PAULA *resumes playing.* CAYLEY *remains* R.C.)

PAULA (*after a pause*). Don't moon about after me, Cayley; follow the others.

DRUMMLE. Thanks, by and by. (*Sitting* R.C. *on ottoman, facing her.*) That's pretty.

PAULA (*after another pause, still playing*). I wish you wouldn't stare so.

DRUMMLE. Was I staring? I'm sorry.

(*He rises and moves to the front of the ottoman ; then glances at* PAULA *and finding her looking at him turns his back. She plays a little longer, then stops suddenly, rises, and goes to the window, where she stands looking out.* DRUMMLE *moves from the ottoman to the settee.*)

(*Quietly.*) A lovely night.

PAULA (*startled*). Oh! (*Without turning to him.*) Why do you hop about like a monkey?

DRUMMLE. Hot rooms play the deuce with the nerves. Now, it would have done you good to have walked in the garden with us after dinner and made merry. Why didn't you?

PAULA (*in a hard voice*). You know why.

DRUMMLE. Ah, you're thinking of the—difference between you and Aubrey?

PAULA. Yes, I *am* thinking of it.

DRUMMLE. Well, so am I. How long——?

PAULA. Getting on for three weeks.

DRUMMLE. Bless me, it must be! And this would have been such a night to have healed it! Moonlight, the stars, the scent of flowers ; and yet enough darkness to enable a kind woman to rest her hand for an instant on the arm of a good fellow who loves her. Ah, ha! it's a wonderful power, dear Mrs. Aubrey, the power of an offended woman! Only realize it! Just that one touch—the mere tips of her fingers—and, for herself and another, she changes the colour of the whole world!

PAULA (*turning to him, calmly*). Cayley, my dear man, you talk exactly like a very romantic old lady.

(*She leaves the window and sits* L.C. *playing with the knick-knacks on the table.*)

DRUMMLE (*to himself, thoughtfully*). H'm, that hasn't done it! (*Rising and coming down.*) Well—ha, ha!—I accept the suggestion. (*Standing beside her.*) An old woman, eh?

PAULA. Oh, I didn't intend——

DRUMMLE. But why not? I've every qualification—well, almost. And I confess it would have given this withered bosom a throb of grandmotherly satisfaction if I could have seen you and Aubrey at peace before I take my leave to-morrow.

PAULA (*looking up quickly*). To-morrow, Cayley!

DRUMMLE. I must.

PAULA. Oh, this house is becoming unendurable.

DRUMMLE. You're very kind. (*Slyly.*) But you've got the Orreyeds.

PAULA (*fiercely*). The Orreyeds! I—I hate the Orreyeds! I lie awake at night, hating them!

DRUMMLE. Pardon me, I've understood that their visit is, in some degree, owing to—hem!—your suggestion.

PAULA. Heavens! that doesn't make me like them better. Somehow or another, I—I've outgrown these people. This woman—I used to think her "jolly!"—sickens me. I can't breathe when she's near me : the whiff of her handkerchief turns me faint! And she patronizes me by the hour, until I—I feel my nails growing longer with every word she speaks!

DRUMMLE. My dear lady, why on earth don't you say all this to Aubrey ?

PAULA. Oh, I've been such an utter fool, Cayley!

DRUMMLE (*soothingly*). Well, well, mention it to Aubrey!

PAULA. No, no, you don't understand. What do you think I've done ?

DRUMMLE. Done ! What, *since* you invited the Orreyeds ?

PAULA. Yes ; I must tell you——

DRUMMLE (*disturbed*). Perhaps you'd better not. (*He moves* R.C.)

PAULA. Look here. I've intercepted some letters from Mrs. Cortelyon and Ellean to—him. (*Producing three unopened letters from the bodice of her dress.*) There are the accursed things ! From Paris—two from the Cortelyon woman, the other from Ellean !

DRUMMLE. But why—why ?

PAULA. I don't know. (*Rising and speaking with great volubility.*) Yes, I do ! I saw letters coming from Ellean to her father ; not a line to me—not a line. And one morning it happened I was downstairs before he was, and I spied this one lying with his heap on the breakfast-table, and I slipped it into my pocket—out of malice, Cayley, pure devilry ! And a day or two afterwards I met Elwes the postman at the Lodge, and took the letters from him, and found these others amongst 'em. I felt simply fiendish when I saw them—fiendish ! (*Returning the letters to her bodice.*) And now I carry them about with me, and they're scorching me like a mustard plaster ! (*She moves up* R.C.)

DRUMMLE. Oh, this accounts for Aubrey not hearing from Paris lately !

PAULA. That's an ingenious conclusion to arrive at ! (*Pacing to and fro excitedly.*) Of course it does ! (*With an hysterical laugh.*) Ha, ha !

DRUMMLE. Well, well ! (*Laughing.*) Ha, ha, ha !

PAULA (*turning upon him*). I suppose it *is* amusing!

DRUMMLE (*with sudden gravity*). I beg pardon.

PAULA. Heaven knows I've little enough to brag about! I'm a bad lot, but not in mean tricks of this sort. (*She moves down* R., *then across the front of the ottoman to* C.) In all my life this is the most caddish thing I've done. How am I to get rid of these letters —that's what I want to know? (*Vehemently.*) How am I to get rid of them?

DRUMMLE. If I were you I should take Aubrey aside and put them into his hands as soon as possible.

PAULA. What! and tell him to his face that I——! No, thank you. (*Hesitatingly.*) I suppose *you* wouldn't like to——

DRUMMLE. No, no; I won't touch 'em! (*He moves to the other side of* L.C. *table.*)

PAULA. And you call yourself my friend?

DRUMMLE (*good-humouredly*). No, I don't!

PAULA. Perhaps I'll tie them together and give them to his man in the morning.

DRUMMLE. That won't avoid an explanation.

PAULA (*recklessly*). Oh, then he must miss them——

DRUMMLE. And trace them.

PAULA (*throwing herself upon the ottoman*, R.C.). I don't care!

DRUMMLE (*smiling and moving back of table*). I know you don't; but (*coaxingly*) let me send him to you now, may I? (*Advancing to her.*)

PAULA. Now! What do you think a woman's made of? I couldn't stand it, Cayley. I haven't slept for nights; and last night there was thunder, too! I believe I've got the horrors.

DRUMMLE (*taking the little hand-mirror from the table* L.C.). You'll sleep well enough when you deliver those letters. (*Going to her.*) Come, come, Mrs. Aubrey—a good night's rest! (*Holding the mirror before her face.*) It's quite time.

(*She looks at herself for a moment, then snatches the mirror from him.*)

PAULA. You brute, Cayley, to show me that! (*She puts it on* R. *seat.*)

DRUMMLE. Then—may I? Be guided by a fr—a poor old woman! May I?

PAULA (*setting her teeth*). You'll kill me, amongst you!

DRUMMLE (*entreatingly*). What do you say?

PAULA (*after a pause*). Very well.

(*He nods his head and goes out rapidly, door up* L. *She looks after him for a moment, and calls "Cayley! Cayley!" Rises and moves* C., *facing audience. Then she again produces the letters, deliberately, one by one, fingering them with aversion. Suddenly she starts, turning her head towards the door.*)

Ah!

(AUBREY *enters quickly, door up* L.)

AUBREY (*coming down on her* L.). Paula!

PAULA (*handing him the letters, her face averted*). There !

(*He examines the letters, puzzled, and looks at her inquiringly.*)

They are many days old. I stole them, I suppose to make you anxious and unhappy.

(*He looks at the letters again, then lays them aside on the table* L.C.)

AUBREY (*gently*). Paula, dear, it doesn't matter.

PAULA (*after a short pause*). Why—why do you take it like this ?

AUBREY. What did you expect ?

PAULA. Oh, but I suppose silent reproaches are really the severest. And then, naturally, you are itching to open your letters. (*She crosses the room to* L.C. *as if to go.*)

AUBREY. Paula ! (*He crosses* R.C.)

(*She pauses.*)

Surely, surely it's all over now ?

PAULA. All over ! (*Mockingly.*) Has my stepdaughter returned then ? When did she arrive ? (*Standing at the door.*) I haven't heard of it !

AUBREY (*quietly*). You can be very cruel.

PAULA. That word's always on a man's lips ; he uses it if his soup's cold. (*With another movement as if to go.*) Need we——

AUBREY. I know I've wounded you, Paula. But isn't there any way out of this ?

PAULA. When does Ellean return ? (*She moves down* L.) To-morrow ? Next week ?

AUBREY (*wearily*). Oh ! Why should we grudge Ellean the little pleasure she is likely to find in Paris and in London. (*He moves* C.)

PAULA. I grudge her nothing, if that's a hit at me. But with that woman——! (*She sits* L. *on the settee.*)

AUBREY. It must be that woman or another. You know that at present we are unable to give Ellean the opportunity of—of——

PAULA. Of mixing with respectable people.

AUBREY. The opportunity of gaining friends, experience, ordinary knowledge of the world. If you are interested in Ellean, can't you see how useful Mrs. Cortelyon's good offices are ?

PAULA (*rising and going to him*). May I put one question ? At the end of the London season, when Mrs. Cortelyon has done with Ellean, is it understood that the girl comes back to us ?

(AUBREY *is silent.*)

Is it ? Is it ?

AUBREY (*hesitatingly*). Let us wait till the end of the season——

PAULA. Oh ! (*She goes down* L.) I knew it. You're only fooling me ; you put me off with any trash. I believe you've sent Ellean away, not for the reasons you give, but because you don't consider me a decent companion for her, because you're afraid she might get a little of her innocence rubbed off in my company. (*She returns to* L. *of him.*) Come, isn't that the truth ? Be honest ! Isn't that it ?

AUBREY. Yes.

(*There is a moment's silence on both sides.*)

PAULA (*with uplifted hands as if to strike him*). Oh !

AUBREY (*taking her by the wrists*). Sit down. Sit down.

(*He puts her into a chair ; she shakes herself free with a cry. From this point to the end of the scene the man dominates.*)

Now listen to me. Fond as you are, Paula, of harking back to your past, there's one chapter of it you always let alone. I've never asked you to speak of it ; you've never offered to speak of it. I mean the chapter that relates to the time when you were—like Ellean.

(*She attempts to rise ; he restrains her.*)

No, no.

PAULA. I don't choose to talk about that time. I won't satisfy your curiosity.

AUBREY. My dear Paula, I have no curiosity—I know what you were at Ellean's age. (*She looks up.*) I'll tell you. You hadn't a thought that wasn't a wholesome one, you hadn't an impulse that didn't tend towards good, you never harboured a notion you couldn't have gossiped about to a parcel of children.

(*She makes another effort to rise : he lays his hand lightly on her shoulder.*)

And this was a very few years back—there are days now when you look like a schoolgirl—but think of the difference between the two Paulas. You'll have to think hard, because after a cruel life one's perceptions grow a thick skin. But, for God's sake, do think till you get these two images clearly in your mind, and then ask yourself what sort of a friend such a woman as you are to-day would have been for the girl of seven or eight years ago.

PAULA (*rising*). How dare you ? I could be almost as good a friend to Ellean as her own mother would have been had she lived. I know what you mean. How dare you ? (*She nearly breaks down.*)

AUBREY. You say that ; very likely you believe it. But you're blind, Paula ; you're blind. You ! Every belief that a young, pure-minded girl holds sacred—that you once held sacred—you now make a target for a jest, a sneer, a paltry cynicism. I tell you, you're not mistress any longer of your thoughts or your tongue. Why, how often, sitting between you and Ellean, have I seen her cheeks turn scarlet as you've rattled off some tale that belongs by right to the club or the smoking-room !

("Oh ! " *from* PAULA.)

Have you noticed the blush ? If you have, has the cause of it ever struck you ? And this is the girl you say you love, I admit that you *do* love, whose love you expect in return ! Oh, Paula, I make the best, the only, excuse for you when I tell you you're blind !

PAULA (*with a restless movement of the hands*). Ellean—Ellean blushes easily.

AUBREY. You blushed as easily a few years ago.

PAULA (*after a short pause*). Well! Have you finished your sermon ?

AUBREY (*with a gesture of despair*). Oh, Paula ! (*He leaves her, going up to the window* R.C. *and standing with his back to the room.*)

PAULA (*to herself*). A few—years ago ! (*She walks slowly towards the door* R., *then suddenly drops upon the ottoman in a paroxysm of weeping.*) O God ! A few years ago !

AUBREY (*going to her*). Paula !

PAULA (*sobbing*). Oh, don't touch me !

AUBREY. Paula !

PAULA. Oh, go away from me !

(*He goes back a few steps to* L.C., *and after a little while she becomes calmer and rises unsteadily ; then in an altered tone.*)

Look here——!

(*He advances a step, front of table ; she checks him with a quick gesture.*)

Look here ! Get rid of these people—Mabel and her husband—as soon as possible ! I—I've done with them ! (*She gets up to the door.*)

AUBREY (*in a whisper*). Paula !

PAULA. And then—then—when the time comes for Ellean to leave Mrs. Cortelyon, give me—give me another chance ! (*He advances again, but she shrinks away.*) No, no !

(*She goes out by the door on the* R. *He sinks on to the settee, covering his eyes with his hands. There is a brief silence, then a* SERVANT *enters, door up* L. AUBREY *looks up quickly.*)

SERVANT. Mrs. Cortelyon, sir, with Miss Ellean.

(AUBREY *rises to meet* MRS. CORTELYON, *who enters, followed by* ELLEAN, *both being in travelling dresses. The* SERVANT *withdraws.*)

MRS. CORTELYON (*shaking hands with* AUBREY C.). Oh, my dear Aubrey ! (*Moves over to* R.C.)

AUBREY. Mrs. Cortelyon ! (*Advancing to and kissing* ELLEAN L.C.) Ellean dear !

ELLEAN. Papa, is all well at home ?

MRS. CORTELYON (R.C.). We're shockingly anxious.

AUBREY. Yes, yes, all's well. This is quite unexpected. (*To* MRS. CORTELYON.) You've found Paris insufferably hot ?

MRS. CORTELYON. Insufferably hot! Paris is pleasant enough. We've had no letter from you!

AUBREY. I wrote to Ellean a week ago.

MRS. CORTELYON. Without alluding to the subject I had written to you upon.

(ELLEAN *goes down* L.)

AUBREY (*thinking*). Ah, of course——

MRS. CORTELYON. And since then we've both written and you've been absolutely silent. Oh, it's too bad!

AUBREY (*picking up the letters from the table,* L.C.). It isn't altogether my fault. Here are the letters——

ELLEAN. Papa! (*She moves up* L. *and over to* MRS. CORTELYON.)

MRS. CORTELYON. They're unopened.

AUBREY. An accident delayed their reaching me till this evening. I'm afraid this has upset you very much. (*He puts letters into his pocket.*)

MRS. CORTELYON (*fretfully*). Upset me!

ELLEAN (*in an undertone to* MRS. CORTELYON, *behind her on* R.). Never mind. Not now, dear—not to-night.

AUBREY. Eh?

MRS. CORTELYON (*to* ELLEAN *aloud*). Child, run away and take your things off. (*Sitting on ottoman.*) She doesn't look as if she'd journeyed from Paris to-day.

(ELLEAN *moves towards the door* L. AUBREY *meets her up* L.C. *and takes her hands.*)

AUBREY. I've never seen her with such a colour.

ELLEAN (*to* AUBREY, *in a faint voice*). Papa, Mrs. Cortelyon has been so very, very kind to me, but I—I have come home.

(*She goes out, door up* L.)

AUBREY (*follows her to door*). Come home! (*To* MRS. CORTELYON, *puzzled.*) Ellean returns to us, then? (*He goes* C.)

MRS. CORTELYON. That's the very point I put to you in my letters, and you oblige me to travel from Paris to Willowmere on a warm day to settle it. I think perhaps it's right that Ellean should be with you just now, although I—— (*In an outburst.*) My dear friend, circumstances are a little altered.

AUBREY. Alice, you're in some trouble. (*He sits* L.C.)

MRS. CORTELYON. Well—yes, I *am* in trouble. You remember pretty little Mrs. Brereton who was once Caroline Ardale?

AUBREY. Quite well.

MRS. CORTELYON. She's a widow now, poor thing. She has the *entresol* of the house where we've been lodging in the Avenue de Friedland. Caroline's a dear chum of mine; she formed a great liking for Ellean. (*Taking off her gloves.*)

AUBREY. I'm very glad.

MRS. CORTELYON. Yes, it's nice for her to meet her mother's friends. Er—that young Hugh Ardale the papers were full of some time ago—he's Caroline Brereton's brother, you know.

AUBREY. No, I didn't know. What did he do ?   I forget.

MRS. CORTELYON. Checked one of those horrid mutinies at some far-away station in India, marched down with a handful of his men and a few faithful natives, and held the place until he was relieved. They gave him his company and a V.C. for it.

AUBREY. And he's Mrs. Brereton's brother ?

MRS. CORTELYON. Yes. He's with his sister—was rather—in Paris. He's home—invalided. (*Impatiently.*)   Good gracious, Aubrey, why don't you help me out ?   Can't you guess what has occurred ?

AUBREY (*quickly*). Alice !

MRS. CORTELYON. Young Ardale—Ellean !

AUBREY (*slowly*). An attachment ?

MRS. CORTELYON. Yes, Aubrey. (*After a little pause.*) Well, I suppose I've got myself into sad disgrace. But really I didn't foresee anything of this kind. A serious, reserved child like Ellean, and a boyish, high-spirited soldier—it never struck me as being likely.

(AUBREY *rises, turns away and paces to and fro thoughtfully, from* R. *to down* L.)

I did all I could directly Captain Ardale spoke—wrote to you at once. Why on earth don't you receive your letters promptly, and when you do get them why can't you open them ?   I endured the anxiety till last night, and then made up my mind—home !   Of course, it has worried me terribly. My head's bursting. Are there any salts about ?

(AUBREY *fetches a bottle from a cabinet and hands it to her.*)

We've had one of those hateful smooth crossings that won't let you be properly indisposed.

AUBREY (*going* C.). My dear Alice, I assure you I've no thought of blaming you.

MRS. CORTELYON. That statement's always precedes a quarrel.

AUBREY. I don't know whether this is the worst or the best luck. How will my wife regard it ?   Is Captain Ardale a good fellow ?

MRS. CORTELYON (*turning to him*). My dear Aubrey, you'd better read up the accounts of his wonderful heroism. Face to face with death for a whole week ; always with a smile and a cheering word for the poor helpless souls depending on him !   Of course, it's that that has stirred the depths of your child's nature. I've watched her while we've been dragging the story out of him, and if angels look different from Ellean at that moment, I don't desire to meet any, that's all !

AUBREY. If you were in my position——?   But you can't judge.

MRS. CORTELYON. Why, if I had a marriageable daughter of my own and Captain Ardale proposed for her, naturally I should cry my eyes out all night—but I should thank Heaven in the morning.

AUBREY. You believe so thoroughly in him ?

MRS. CORTELYON (*laying her hand on* AUBREY'S *arm*). Do you think I should have only a headache at this minute if I didn't ! Look here, you've got to see me down the lane ; that's the least you can do, my friend. (*She moves up* C.) Come into my house for a moment and shake hands with Hugh.

AUBREY. What, is he here ?

MRS. CORTELYON. He came through with us, to present himself formally to-morrow. Where are my gloves ?

(AUBREY *fetches them from the ottoman, and hands them to her*.)

Make my apologies to Mrs. Tanqueray, please. She's well, I hope ? (*Going towards the door up* L.) I can't feel sorry she hasn't seen me in this condition.

(ELLEAN *enters, door up* L.)

ELLEAN (*to* MRS. CORTELYON). I've been waiting to wish you good night. I was afraid I'd missed you.

MRS. CORTELYON. Good night, Ellean.

ELLEAN (*in a low voice, embracing* MRS. CORTELYON). I can't thank you. Dear Mrs. Cortelyon !

MRS. CORTELYON (*her arms round* ELLEAN, *in a whisper to* AUBREY). Speak a word to her.

(MRS. CORTELYON *goes out, door up* L.)

AUBREY (*to* ELLEAN). Ellean, I'm going to see Mrs. Cortelyon home. (*Going to the door.*) Tell Paula where I am ; explain, dear.

ELLEAN (*her head drooping*). Yes. (*She moves* R.C.—*quickly.*) Father ! (*He turns to her.*) You are angry with me—disappointed ?

AUBREY. Angry ?—no.

ELLEAN. Disappointed ?

AUBREY (*gently smiling, going to her and taking her hand*). If so, it's only because you've shaken my belief in my discernment. I thought you took after your poor mother a little, Ellean ; (*looking into her face earnestly*) but there's a look on your face to-night, dear, that I never saw on hers—never, never.

ELLEAN (*leaning her head on his shoulder—tearfully*). Perhaps I ought not to have gone away ?

AUBREY. Hush ! You're quite happy ?

ELLEAN. Yes.

AUBREY. That's right. Then, as you are quite happy there is something I particularly want you to do for me, Ellean.

ELLEAN. What is that ?

AUBREY. Be very gentle with Paula. Will you ?

(*She releases herself.*)

ELLEAN (*slowly*). You think I have been unkind.

AUBREY (*kissing her upon the forehead*). Be very gentle with Paula.

(*He goes out door up* L., *and she stands* C. *looking after him. A rose is thrown through the window and falls at her feet. She picks up the flower wonderingly and goes to the window.*)

ELLEAN (*starting back*). Hugh!

(HUGH ARDALE, *a handsome young man of about seven-and-twenty, with a boyish face and manner, appears outside the window.*)

HUGH. Nelly! Nelly dear!

ELLEAN (*alarmed*). What's the matter?

HUGH. Hush! Nothing. It's only fun. (*Laughing.*) Ha, ha, ha! I've found out that Mrs. Cortelyon's meadow runs up to your father's plantation; I've come through a gap in the hedge.

(*He remains at the window* R.C.)

ELLEAN. Why, Hugh?

HUGH. I'm miserable at The Warren; it's so different from the Avenue de Friedland.

(ELLEAN *moves down to* C.)

Don't look like that! Upon my word I meant just to peep at your home and go back, but I saw figures moving about here, and came nearer, hoping to get a glimpse of you. (*Coming down* C.) Was that your father?

ELLEAN (*moving up to* L. *window*). Yes.

HUGH. Isn't this fun! A rabbit ran across my foot while I was hiding behind that old yew.

ELLEAN (*going down* L.C.). You must go away; it's not *right* for you to be here like this.

HUGH. But it's only fun, I tell you. You take everything so seriously. Do wish me good night.

ELLEAN. We have said good night.

HUGH. In the hall at The Warren, before Mrs. Cortelyon and a man-servant. Oh, it's so different from the Avenue de Friedland!

ELLEAN (*moving to him, giving him her hand hastily*). Good night, Hugh.

HUGH. Is that all? We might be the merest acquaintances.

(*He momentarily embraces her, but she releases herself.*)

ELLEAN. It's when you're like this that you make me feel utterly miserable. (*Throwing the rose from her angrily.*) Oh! (*She moves* L.)

HUGH (*drawing back*). I've offended you now, I suppose?

ELLEAN. Yes.

HUGH. Forgive me, Nelly. Come into the garden for five minutes; we'll stroll down to the plantation.

ELLEAN. No, no.

HUGH. For two minutes—to tell me you forgive me.

ELLEAN. I forgive you.

HUGH. Evidently. (*He moves up to* R.C. *window.*) I shan't sleep a wink to-night after this.

(ELLEAN *moves up to* R. *door.*)

What a fool I am! (*Entreatively.*) Come down to the plantation. Make it up with me.

ELLEAN. There is somebody coming into this room. (*Holding door-handle.*) Do you wish to be seen here?

HUGH (*hurriedly*). I shall wait for you behind that yew-tree. You *must* speak to me. Nelly!

(*He disappears off* L. ELLEAN *goes to* L.C. *window as* PAULA *enters door* R.)

PAULA (*with joyful surprise*). Ellean!

ELLEAN. You—you are very surprised to see me, Paula, of course.

PAULA. Why are you here? Why aren't you with—your friend? (*Contemptuously.*)

ELLEAN. I've come home—if you'll have me. We left Paris this morning; Mrs. Cortelyon brought me back. She was here a minute or two ago; Papa has just gone with her to The Warren. He asked me to tell you.

PAULA (*moving down* R.C.). There are some people staying with us that I'd rather you didn't meet. It was hardly worth your while to return for a few hours.

ELLEAN. A few hours? (*She goes down* C.)

PAULA. Well, when do you go to London?

ELLEAN. I don't think I go to London, after all.

PAULA (*eagerly*). You—you've quarrelled with her? (*She moves to her.*)

ELLEAN (*moving to back of the chair*). No, no, no, not that; but—Paula! (*In an altered tone.*) Paula!

PAULA (*startled*). Eh?

(ELLEAN *goes deliberately to* PAULA *and kisses her.*)

(*Breathlessly,* R.C.) Ellean!

ELLEAN. Kiss *me.*

PAULA. What—what's come to you?

ELLEAN. I want to behave differently to you in the future. Is it too late?

PAULA. Too—late! (*Impulsively kissing* ELLEAN *and crying.*) No—no—no! No—no!

ELLEAN. Paula, don't cry.

PAULA (*wiping her eyes*). I'm a little shaky; I haven't been sleeping. It's all right—talk to me.

ELLEAN (*hesitatingly*). There is something I want to tell you——

PAULA. Is there—is there ?

(*They sit together on the ottoman,* R.O., PAULA *taking* ELLEAN'S *hand.*)

ELLEAN. Paula, in our house in the Avenue de Friedland, on the floor below us, there was a Mrs. Brereton. She used to be a friend of my mother's. Mrs. Cortelyon and I spent a great deal of our time with her.

PAULA (*suspiciously*). Oh ! (*Letting* ELLEAN'S *hand fall.*) Is this lady going to take you up in place of Mrs. Cortelyon ?

ELLEAN. No, no. (*Falteringly.*) Her brother is staying with her—*was* staying with her. Her brother—— (*She breaks off in confusion.*)

PAULA (*looking into her face*). Well ?

ELLEAN (*almost inaudibly*). Paula——

(*She rises and walks away to* L.C., PAULA *following her.*)

PAULA. Ellean ! (*Taking hold of her.*) You're not in love !

(ELLEAN *looks at* PAULA *appealingly.*)

Oh ! *You* in love ! You ! (*Suspiciously.*) Oh, this is why you've come home ! Of course, you can make friends with me now ! You'll leave us for good soon, I suppose ; so it doesn't much matter being civil to me for a little while ! (*She goes round the front of the ottoman to the piano, where she stands facing* ELLEAN.)

ELLEAN. Oh, Paula !

PAULA. Why, how you have deceived us—all of us ! We've taken you for a cold-blooded little saint. The fools you've made of us ! (*Bitterly.*) Saint Ellean ! Saint Ellean !

ELLEAN (*passionately*). Ah, I might have known you'd only mock me ! (*She goes up* C. *to the settee.*)

PAULA (*her tone changing*). Eh ?

ELLEAN (R.C., *turning away*). I—I can't talk to you. (*Sitting on the settee.*) You do nothing else but mock and sneer, nothing else. (*She crys.*)

PAULA (*to* C.—*following her penitently*). Ellean dear ! Ellean ! I didn't mean it. I'm so horribly jealous, it's a sort of curse on me. (*Kneeling beside* ELLEAN *and embracing her.*) My tongue runs away with me. I'm going to alter, I swear I am. I've made some good resolutions, and, as God's above me, I'll keep them ! If you *are* in love, if you *do* ever marry, that's no reason why we shouldn't be fond of each other. Come, you've kissed me of your own accord —you can't take it back. Now we're friends again, aren't we ? Ellean dear ! I want to know everything, everything. Ellean dear, Ellean !

ELLEAN. Paula, Hugh has done something that makes me very angry. He came with us from Paris to-day, to see Papa. He is staying with Mrs. Cortelyon and—(*She rises and goes down* R.C.) I ought to tell you——

PAULA. Yes, yes. What ? (*She rises and remains up* L.C.)

ELLEAN. He has found his way by The Warren meadow through the plantation up to this house. He is waiting to bid me good night. (*Glancing towards the garden.*) He is—out there.

PAULA (*pleased*). Oh !

ELLEAN. What shall I do ?

PAULA (*moving to her*). Bring him in to see me ! Will you ?

ELLEAN. No, no.

PAULA. But I'm dying to know him. Oh, yes, you must. I shall meet him before Aubrey does. (*Coming down excitedly to table* L.C., *running her hands over her hair.*) I'm so glad.

(ELLEAN *goes out by the window* L.C.)

The mirror—mirror. What a fright I must look ! (*Not finding the hand-glass on the table, she jumps on to the settee* L., *and surveys herself in the mirror over the mantelpiece, then returns to* L.C. *chair and sits quietly down and waits.*) Ellean ! Just fancy ! Ellean !

(*After a pause* ELLEAN *enters by the window* L.C. *with* HUGH.)

ELLEAN (C.). Paula, this is Captain Ardale—Mrs. Tanqueray.

(PAULA *rises and turns, and she and* HUGH *stand staring blankly at each other for a moment or two ; then* PAULA *advances and gives him her hand.*)

PAULA (*in a strange voice, but calmly*). How do you do ?

HUGH. How do you do ?

PAULA (*to* ELLEAN). Mr. Ardale and I have met in London, Ellean. Er—Captain Ardale, now ?

HUGH. Yes.

ELLEAN (L.C., *simply*). In London ?

PAULA. They say the world's very small, don't they ?

HUGH. Yes.

PAULA. Ellean, dear, I want to have a little talk about you to Mr. Ardale—Captain Ardale—alone. (*Putting her arms round* ELLEAN, *and leading her to the door* L.) Come back in a little while.

(ELLEAN *nods to* PAULA *with a smile and goes out, while* PAULA *stands watching her at the open door.*)

In a little while—in a little—— (*Closing the door and coming down to* L.C. *and then taking a seat facing* HUGH, *who has not moved.*) Be quick ! Mr. Tanqueray has only gone down to The Warren with Mrs. Cortelyon. What is to be done ?

HUGH (*blankly*). Done ? (*He puts his hat on the ottoman.*)

PAULA (*sitting in chair* L.). Done—done. (*Holding her brow.*) Something must be done. (*With great force.*)

HUGH. I understand that Mr. Tanqueray had married a Mrs.— Mrs.——

PAULA. Jarman ?

HUGH. Yes.

PAULA. I'd been going by that name. You didn't follow my doings after we separated.

HUGH. No.

PAULA (*sneeringly*). No.

HUGH. I went out to India.

PAULA. What's to be done?

HUGH. Damn this chance! (*He goes down* R., *and up round the ottoman.*)

PAULA (*bowing her head*). Oh, my God!

HUGH (*back to* C.). Your husband doesn't know, does he?

PAULA. That you and I——?

HUGH. Yes.

PAULA. No. He knows about others.

HUGH. Not about me. How long were we——?

PAULA. I don't remember, exactly.

HUGH. Do you—do you think it matters?

PAULA. His—his daughter.

(*With a muttered exclamation he turns away and sits up* C., *with his head in his hands.*)

What's to be done?

HUGH. I wish I could think.

PAULA (*ramblingly*). Oh! Oh! What happened to that flat of ours in Ethelbert Street? (*She mechanically pushes her hair back from her left temple.*)

HUGH. I let it.

PAULA. All that pretty furniture?

HUGH. Sold it.

PAULA. I came across the key of the escritoire the other day in an old purse! (*The three lines preceding she has sat quite quietly and retrospectively. Suddenly realizing the horror and hopelessness of her position, and starting to her feet with an hysterical cry of rage.*) What am I maundering about? (*She strides across in front of the ottoman to the piano.*)

HUGH. For God's sake, be quiet! Do let me think.

PAULA (*pacing up to* R.). This will send me mad! (*Suddenly turning and standing over him.*) You—you beast, to crop up in my life again like this!

HUGH (*rising, facing her*). I always treated you fairly.

PAULA (*weakly*). Oh! I beg your pardon—I know you did—I——

(*She sinks on to the chair up* C., *crying hysterically.*)

HUGH. Hush! (*He goes to her.*)

PAULA. She kissed me to-night! I'd won her over! I've had such a fight to make her love me! And now—just as she's beginning to love me, to bring this on her!

Hugh. Hush, hush! Don't break down! (*He is apprehensive of someone coming into the room.*)

Paula (*sobbing*). You don't know! I—I haven't been getting on well in my marriage. It's been my fault. The life I used to lead spoilt me completely. But I'd made up my mind to turn over a new life from to-night. From to-night!

Hugh. Paula——

Paula. Don't you call me that! (*She staggers down to* l.c. *chair.*)

Hugh. Mrs. Tanqueray, there is no cause for you to despair in this way. It's all right, I tell you—it *shall* be all right.

Paula (*shivering*). What are we to do? (*She sits* l.c.)

Hugh. Hold our tongues. (*He moves down* c.)

Paula (*staring vacantly*). Eh?

Hugh. The chances are a hundred to one against any one ever turning up who knew us when we were together. Besides, no one would be such a brute as to split on us. If anybody did do such a thing we should have to lie! What are we upsetting ourselves like this for, when we've simply got to hold our tongues?

Paula. You're as mad *as* I am!

Hugh. Can you think of a better plan?

Paula. There's only one plan possible—(*rising*) let's come to our senses!—Mr. Tanqueray must be told. (*She crosses* r.)

Hugh. Your husband! What, and I lose Ellean! I lose Ellean!

Paula (r.). You've *got* to lose her.

Hugh (c.). I *won't* lose her! I *can't* lose her! (*He moves up* l.c.)

Paula (r.). Didn't I read of your doing any number of brave things in India? Why, you seem to be an awful coward!

Hugh. That's another sort of pluck altogether—(*coming* c.) I haven't this sort of pluck.

Paula. Oh, I don't ask *you* to tell Mr. Tanqueray. (*Determinedly.*) That's my job. (*She sits on the front seat of the ottoman.*)

Hugh (*crossing to her*). You—you—you'd better! You——!

Paula (*rising*). Don't bully me! I intend to.

Hugh (*taking hold of her; she wrenches herself free*). Look here, Paula! I never treated you badly—you've owned it. Why should you want to pay me out like this? You don't know how I love Ellean!

Paula. Yes, that's just what I *do* know. (*She crosses* l.c. *and sits.*)

Hugh. I say you don't! (*Turning to her.*) She's as good as my own mother. I've been downright honest with her too. I told her, in Paris, that I'd been a bit wild at one time, and, after a damned wretched day, she promised to forgive me because of what I'd done since in India. She's behaved like an angel to me! Surely I oughtn't to lose her, after all, just because I've been like other fellows! No; I haven't been half as rackety as a hundred men we could think of. (*He tries to take her hands.*) Paula, don't pay me out for nothing ; be fair to me, there's a good girl—be fair to me !

PAULA (*crossing to* L.C.). Oh, I'm not considering you at all ! I advise you not to stay here any longer ; Mr. Tanqueray is sure to be back soon.

HUGH (*taking up his hat and staggering up* R.C.). What's the understanding between us then ? What have we arranged to do ?

PAULA. I don't know what you're going to do. (*She moves down* L.C.) I've got to tell Mr. Tanqueray.

HUGH (*approaching her fiercely*). By God, you shall do nothing of the sort !

PAULA. You shocking coward !

HUGH. If you dare ! (*Going up to the window* R.C.) Mind ! If you dare !

PAULA (*following him*). Why, what would you do ?

HUGH (*after a short pause, sullenly*). Nothing. I'd shoot myself —that's nothing. Good night.

PAULA. Good night.

(*He disappears. She walks unsteadily to the ottoman, and sits ; and as she does so her hand falls upon the little silver mirror, which she takes up, staring at her own reflection.*)

The CURTAIN *falls.*

ACT IV

The drawing-room at " Highercombe," the same evening.

PAULA *is still seated on the ottoman, looking vacantly before her, with the little mirror in her hand.* LADY ORREYED *enters, door* L.

LADY ORREYED. There you are! You never came into the billiard-room. Isn't it maddening—Cayley Drummle gives me sixty out of a hundred and beats me. I must be out of form, because I know I play remarkably well for a lady. (*Going to her.*) Only last month——

(PAULA *rises.*)

Whatever is the matter with you, old girl?
PAULA. Why?
LADY ORREYED (*staring*). It's the light, I suppose.

(PAULA *crosses to* L.C. *and replaces the mirror on the table.*)

By Aubrey's bolting from the billiard-table in that fashion I thought perhaps——
PAULA. Yes; it's all right.
LADY ORREYED. You've patched it up?

(PAULA *nods.*)

(*Going to her.*) Oh, I am jolly glad——! (*Kisses her.*) I mean——
PAULA. Yes, I know what you mean. Thanks, Mabel.
LADY ORREYED. Now take my advice; for the future——
PAULA (*abruptly*). Mabel, if I've been disagreeable to you while you've been staying here, I—I beg your pardon. (*She walks away and sits up* R.C.)
LADY ORREYED. You disagreeable, my dear? I haven't noticed it. Dodo and me both consider you make a first-class hostess, but then you've had such practice, haven't you? (*Dropping on to the ottoman and gaping.*) Oh, talk about being sleepy——!
PAULA. Why don't you——!
LADY ORREYED. Why, dear, I must hang about for Dodo. You may as well know it; he's in one of his moods. (*She rises and joins* PAULA, *sitting on her* R.)
PAULA (*under her breath*). Oh——!
LADY ORREYED. Now, it's not his fault; it was deadly dull for him while we were playing billiards. Cayley Drummle did ask him to mark, but I stopped that; it's so easy to make a gentleman

60

look like a billiard-marker. This is just how it always is ; if poor
old Dodo has nothing to do, he loses count, as you may say.

PAULA.   Hark !

(SIR GEORGE ORREYED *enters, door* L., *walking slowly and deliberately ;
he looks pale and watery-eyed.*)

SIR GEORGE (*with mournful indistinctness*).   I'm 'fraid we've lef'
you a grea' deal to yourself to-night, Mrs. Tanqueray.   Attra'tions
of billiards. I apol'gize. (*He staggers gentlemanly down* L.C. *to chair.*)
I say, where's ol' Aubrey ?

PAULA (*without turning*).   My husband has been obliged to go
out to a neighbour's house. (*She rises and goes to the window.*)

SIR GEORGE.   I want his advice on a rather pressing matter
connected with my family—my family. (*Sitting.*)   To-morrow will
do just as well.

LADY ORREYED (*aside to* PAULA).   This is the mood I hate so—
drivelling about his precious family.

SIR GEORGE.   The fact is, Mrs. Tanqueray, I am not easy in
my min' 'bout the way I am treatin' my poor ol' mother.

LADY ORREYED (*to* PAULA).   Do you hear that ?   That's *his*
mother, but *my* mother he won't so much as look at !

SIR GEORGE.   I shall write to Bruton Street firs' thing in the
morning.

LADY ORREYED (*to* PAULA).   Mamma has stuck to me through
everything—well, you know ! (*Coming down* R.C.)

SIR GEORGE.   I'll get ol' Aubrey to figure out a letter. I'll drop
a line to Uncle Fitz too—dooced shame of the ol' feller to chuck
me over in this manner. (*Wiping his eyes.*)   All my family have
chucked me over.

LADY ORREYED (*rising*).   Dodo ! (*She moves down* C.)

SIR GEORGE.   Jus' because I've married beneath me, to be
chucked over ! (*Counting them on his fingers.*)   Aunt Lydia, the
General, Hooky Whitgrave, Lady Sugnall—my own dear sister !
—all turn their backs on me. It's more than I can stan' !

LADY ORREYED (*approaching nearer to him with dignity*).   Sir
George, wish Mrs. Tanqueray good night at once and come upstairs.
Do you hear me ?

SIR GEORGE (*rising angrily*).   Wha'——

LADY ORREYED.   Be quiet !

SIR GEORGE.   You presoom to order me about !

LADY ORREYED.   You're making an exhibition of yourself !

(PAULA *rises.*)

SIR GEORGE.   Look 'ere——!

LADY ORREYED.   Come along, I tell you !

(*He hesitates, utters a few inarticulate sounds, then snatches up a
fragile ornament from the table, and is about to dash it on to the*

ground. LADY ORREYED *retreats.* PAULA *comes down, and taking the ornament from him places it upon mantelshelf.*)

PAULA (c.). George!

(*He shakes* PAULA'S *hand.*)

SIR GEORGE. Good ni', Mrs. Tanqueray.

LADY ORREYED (*to* PAULA). Good night, darling. Wish Aubrey good night for me. Now, Dodo? (*The first two sentences she says with affected sweetness, the last with great severity.*)

(*She goes out, door* R.)

SIR GEORGE (*to* PAULA). I say, are you goin' to sit up for ol' Aubrey?

PAULA. Yes.

SIR GEORGE. Shall I keep you comp'ny?

PAULA. No, thank you, George.

SIR GEORGE. Sure?

PAULA. Yes, sure.

SIR GEORGE (*shaking hands*). Good night again.

PAULA. Good night.

(*She turns away. He goes out, steadying himself carefully, door* R. DRUMMLE *appears outside the window* L.C., *with a cap on his head and smoking.*)

DRUMMLE (*looking into the room, and seeing* PAULA). My last cigar. Where's Aubrey?

PAULA. Gone down to The Warren, to see Mrs. Cortelyon home.

DRUMMLE (*entering the room*). Eh? Did you say Mrs. Cortelyon?

PAULA. Yes. She has brought Ellean back.

DRUMMLE. Bless my soul! Why?

PAULA (R.C.). I—I'm too tired to tell you, Cayley. If you stroll along the lane you'll meet Aubrey. (*Sitting* R.C.) Get the news from him.

DRUMMLE (*going up to the window*). Yes, yes. (*Returning to* PAULA.) I don't want to bother you, only—the anxious old woman, you know. Are you and Aubrey——?

PAULA. Good friends again?

DRUMMLE (*nodding*). Um.

PAULA (*giving him her hand*). Quite, Cayley, quite.

DRUMMLE (*retaining her hand*). That's capital. As I'm off so early to-morrow morning, let me say now—thank you for your hospitality.

(*He bends over her hand gallantly, then goes out by the window, up* L.C.)

PAULA (*to herself*). "Are you and Aubrey——?" "Good friends again?" "Yes." "Quite, Cayley, quite."

(*There is a brief pause, then* AUBREY *enters hurriedly, door* L., *wearing a light overcoat and carrying a cap.*)

AUBREY. Paula dear ! Have you seen Ellean ? (*Standing* o.)
PAULA. I found her here when I came down.
AUBREY. She—she's told you ?
PAULA. Yes, Aubrey.
AUBREY. It's extraordinary, isn't it ! Not that somebody should fall in love with Ellean or that Ellean herself should fall in love. All that's natural enough and was bound to happen, I suppose, sooner or later. But this young fellow ! You know his history ?
PAULA (*startled*). His history ?
AUBREY. You remember the papers were full of his name a few months ago ?
PAULA. Oh, yes.
AUBREY. The man's as brave as a lion, there's no doubt about that ; and, at the same time, he's like a big good-natured schoolboy, Mrs. Cortelyon says. Have you ever pictured the kind of man Ellean would marry some day ?
PAULA. I can't say that I have.
AUBREY. A grave, sedate fellow I've thought about—hah ! She has fallen in love with the way in which Ardale practically laid down his life to save those poor people shut up in the Residency. (*Taking off his coat.*) Well, I suppose if a man can do that sort of thing, one ought to be content. And yet—— (*Throwing his coat on the settee.*) I should have met him to-night, but he'd gone out. (*Coming down to her.*) Paula dear, tell me how you look upon this business. (*To chair* L.C. *and sitting.*)
PAULA. Yes, I will—I must. To begin with, I—I've seen Mr. Ardale.

(*He rises and goes to her.*)

AUBREY. Captain Ardale ?
PAULA. Captain Ardale.
AUBREY. Seen him ?
PAULA. While you were away he came up here, through our grounds, to try to get a word with Ellean. I made her fetch him in and present him to me.
AUBREY (*frowning*). Doesn't Captain Ardale know there's a lodge and a front door to this place ? Never mind ! What is your impression of him ?
PAULA. Aubrey, do you recollect my bringing you a letter—a letter giving you an account of myself—to the Albany late one night—the night before we got married ?
AUBREY. A letter ?
PAULA. You burnt it ; don't you know ?
AUBREY. Yes ; I know. (*Rises and goes to her.*)
PAULA. His name was in that letter.
AUBREY (*going back from her slowly, and staring at her*). I don't understand.

PAULA (*with forced calmness*).   Well—Ardale and I once kept house together.

(*He remains silent, not moving.*)

(*After a pause.*)   Why don't you strike me ?   Hit me in the face —I'd rather you did !   Hurt me !   hurt me !   (*She screams and nearly swoons.*)

AUBREY (*after a pause*).   What did you—and this man—say to each other—just now ?

PAULA.   I—hardly—know.

AUBREY.   Think !

PAULA.   The end of it all was that I—I told him I must inform you of—what had happened . . . he didn't want me to do that . . . I declared I would . . . he dared me to.

(AUBREY *advances a step and bends over her.*)

(*Breaking down.*)   Let me alone !—oh !

AUBREY.   Where was my daughter while this went on ?

PAULA.   I—I had sent her out of the room . . . that is all right.

AUBREY.   Yes, yes—yes, yes.

(*Click of lock heard.   He turns his head towards the door,* L.)

PAULA (*nervously*).   Who's that ?

(*He goes to the door, meeting a* SERVANT *who enters with a letter.*)

SERVANT.   The coachman has just run up with this from The Warren, sir.

(AUBREY *takes the letter.*)

It's for Mrs. Tanqueray, sir ; there's no answer.

(*The* SERVANT *withdraws.*   AUBREY *goes to* PAULA *and drops the letter into her lap ; she opens it with uncertain hands.*   AUBREY *moves* C.)

PAULA (*reading it to herself*).   It's from—him.   (*Long pause.*) He's going away—or gone—I think.   (*Rising in a weak way.*) What does it say ?   I never could make out his writing.

(*She gives the letter to* AUBREY *and stands near him looking at the letter over his shoulder as he reads.   Letter to be written on two sides.*)

AUBREY (*reading*).   "I shall be in Paris by to-morrow evening. Shall wait there, at Meurice's, for a week, ready to receive any communication you or your husband may address to me.   Please invent some explanation to Ellean.   Mrs. Tanqueray, for God's sake, do what you can for me."

(PAULA *and* AUBREY *speak in low voices, both still looking at the letter.*)

PAULA.   Has he left The Warren, I wonder, already ?

AUBREY.   That doesn't matter.

PAULA. No, but I can picture him going quietly off. Very likely he's walking on to Bridgeford or Cottering to-night, to get the first train in the morning. A pleasant stroll for him.

AUBREY. We'll reckon he's gone, that's enough.

PAULA. That isn't to be answered in any way ?

AUBREY. Silence will answer that.

PAULA. He'll soon recover his spirits, I know.

AUBREY. You know. (*Offering her the letter.*) You don't want this, I suppose ?

PAULA. No.

AUBREY. It's done with—done with.

(*He tears the letter into small pieces. She has dropped the envelope ; she searches for it, finds it, and gives it to him.*)

PAULA. Here !

AUBREY (*looking at the remnants of the letter*). This is no good ; I must burn it.

PAULA. Burn it in your room.

AUBREY. Yes. (*Passively.*)

PAULA. Put it in your pocket for now.

AUBREY (L. *in front of table*). Yes.

(*He does so. ELLEAN enters door R., comes down R. of settee, and they both turn, guiltily, and stare at her.*)

ELLEAN (*after a short silence, wonderingly*). Papa——

AUBREY. What do you want, Ellean ?

ELLEAN (*moves down* R.). I heard from Willis that you had come in ; I only want to wish you good night.

(PAULA *steals away, door* R. *without looking back.*)

(*Puzzled.*) What's the matter ?

(*She crosses* C., *front of the ottoman, to* AUBREY.)

Ah ! (*her head drooping.*) Of course, Paula has told you about Captain Ardale ?

AUBREY. Well ?

ELLEAN (*falteringly*). Have you and he met ?

AUBREY. No.

ELLEAN. You are angry with him ; (*laying her hand on his arm*) so was I. But to-morrow when he calls and express his regret—to-morrow——

AUBREY. Ellean—Ellean !

ELLEAN. Yes, Papa ?

AUBREY. I—I can't let you see this man again. (*He walks away from her up stage* R.C., *in a paroxysm of distress, then, after a moment or two, he returns to her and takes her to his arms.*) Ellean ! my child !

ELLEAN (*releasing herself*). What has happened, Papa ? What is it ?

AUBREY (*thinking out his words deliberately*). Something has occurred, something has come to my knowledge, in relation to Captain Ardale, which puts any further acquaintanceship between you two out of the question.

ELLEAN. Any further acquaintanceship . . . out of the question ?

AUBREY. Yes.

(*She sits* L.C. *He advances to her quickly, but she shrinks from him.*)

ELLEAN. No, no—I am quite well. (*After a short pause.*) It's not an hour ago since Mrs. Cortelyon left you and me together here ; you had nothing to urge against Captain Ardale then.

AUBREY. No.

ELLEAN. You don't know each other ; you haven't even seen him this evening. Father !

AUBREY (*firmly*). I have told you he and I have not met.

ELLEAN (*in chair*). Mrs. Cortelyon couldn't have spoken against him to you just now. No, no, no ; she's too good a friend to both of us. (*Turning to him.*) Aren't you going to give me some explanation ? You can't take this position towards me—towards Captain Ardale—without affording me the fullest explanation.

AUBREY (*with difficulty, next to her*). Ellean, there are circumstances connected with Captain Ardale's career which you had better remain ignorant of. It must be sufficient for you that I consider these circumstances render him unfit to be your husband.

ELLEAN. Father !

AUBREY. You must trust me, Ellean ; you must try to understand the depth of my love for you and the—the agony it gives me to hurt you. You must trust me. (*He moves* R.C.)

ELLEAN (*she rises and goes to him composedly*). I will, Father ; but you must trust me a little too. Circumstances connected with Captain Ardale's career ?

AUBREY. Yes.

ELLEAN. When he presents himself here to-morrow of course you will see him and let him defend himself ?

AUBREY. Captain Ardale will not be here to-morrow.

ELLEAN (*after a pause*). Not ! You have stopped his coming here ?

AUBREY. Indirectly—yes.

ELLEAN. But just now he was talking to me at that window ! Nothing had taken place then ! And since then nothing can have——! (*Suddenly.*) Oh ! Why—you have heard something against him from Paula.

AUBREY. From—Paula !

ELLEAN. She knows him.

AUBREY. She has told you so ?

ELLEAN. When I introduced Captain Ardale to her she said she had met him in London. Of course ! It is Paula who has done this !

AUBREY (*crossing to her* c.—*in a hard voice*). I—I hope you— you'll refrain from rushing at conclusions. There's nothing to be gained by trying to avoid the main point, which is that you must drive Captain Ardale out of your thoughts. Understand that! You're able to obtain comfort from your religion, aren't you? I'm glad to think that's so. I talk to you in a harsh way, Ellean, but I feel your pain almost as acutely as you do. (*Going to the door up* L.) I—I can't say anything more to you to-night.

ELLEAN (*turning* R.C.). Father!

(*He pauses at the door.*)

Father, I'm obliged to ask you this; there's no help for it—I've no mother to go to. Does what you have heard about Captain Ardale concern the time when he led a wild, a dissolute life in London?

AUBREY (*returning to her slowly and staring at her*). Explain yourself! (*To* c. *behind table.*)

ELLEAN. He has been quite honest with me. One day—in Paris—he confessed to me—what a man's life is—what his life had been.

AUBREY (*under his breath*). Oh!

ELLEAN (*tearfully*). He offered to go away, not to approach me again.

AUBREY. And you—you accepted his view of what a man's life is!

ELLEAN. As far as *I* could forgive him, I forgave him.

AUBREY (*with a groan*). Why, when was it you left us? It hasn't taken you long to get your robe "just a little dusty at the hem!"

ELLEAN. What do you mean?

AUBREY. Hah! A few weeks ago my one great desire was to keep you ignorant of evil.

ELLEAN. Father, it is impossible to be ignorant of evil. Instinct, common instinct, teaches us what is good and bad. Surely I am none the worse for knowing what is wicked and detesting it!

AUBREY. *Detesting* it! Why, you *love* this fellow! (*He sits* L.C.)

ELLEAN. Ah, you don't understand! (*She delivers this speech standing* R. *of* L.C. *chair, whereon* AUBREY *is seated.*) I have simply judged Captain Ardale as we all pray to be judged. I have lived in imagination through that one week in India when he deliberately offered his life back to God to save those wretched, desperate people. In his whole career I see now nothing but that one week; those few hours bring him nearer the Saints, I believe, than fifty uneventful years of mere blamelessness would have done! (*Down* R.) And so, Father, if Paula has reported anything to Captain Ardale's discredit—— (*She moves* R.C.)

AUBREY (*rising and going to her*). Paula——!

ELLEAN. It *must* be Paula; it can't be anybody else.

AUBREY. You—you'll please keep Paula out of the question. Finally, Ellean, understand me—I have made up my mind.

(*Again going to the door up* L. *She follows him.*)

ELLEAN. But wait—listen! (*She goes up* R.C.) I have made up my mind also.

AUBREY (*facing her*). Ah! I recognize your mother in you now!

ELLEAN (*quickly*). You need not speak against my mother because you are angry with me!

AUBREY (*unsteadily*). I—I hardly know what I'm saying to you. In the morning—in the morning—— (*Moves to the door.*)

(*He goes out. Suddenly she turns her head to listen. Then, after a moment's hesitation, she goes softly to the window* R.C., *and looks out under the verandah.*)

ELLEAN (*in a whisper*). Paula! Paula!

(PAULA *appears outside the window and steps into the room ; her face is white and drawn, her hair is a little disordered.*)

PAULA (*huskily*). Well?

ELLEAN. Have you been under the verandah all the while—listening?

PAULA. N—no.

ELLEAN. You *have* overheard us—I see you have. And it *is* you who have been speaking to my father against Captain Ardale. Isn't it? (*Down* L.) Paula, why don't you own it or deny it?

PAULA (*faintly*). Oh, I—I don't mind owning it ; why should I?

ELLEAN. Ah! You seem to have been very, very eager to tell your tale.

PAULA. No, I wasn't eager, Ellean. I'd have given something not to have had to do it. I wasn't eager.

ELLEAN. Not! Oh, I think you might safely have spared us all for a little while. (*She crosses back of table to the* L. *settee.*)

PAULA. But, Ellean, you forget I—I am your stepmother. It was my—my duty—to tell your father what I—what I knew——

ELLEAN. What you knew! Why, after all, what can you know! You can only speak from gossip, report, hearsay! How is it possible that you——!

(*She stops abruptly and moves over to* PAULA. *The two women stand staring at each other for a moment ; then* ELLEAN *backs away from* PAULA *slowly.*)

Paula!

PAULA (*advancing*). What—what's the matter?

ELLEAN. You—you knew Captain Ardale in London!

PAULA. Why—what do you mean?

ELLEAN. Oh!

(*She makes for the door* R., *but* PAULA *turns and catches her by the wrist.* ELLEAN *is now* R.C., PAULA C.)

PAULA.   You shall tell me what you mean!

ELLEAN (*helplessly*).   Ah! (*Suddenly looking fixedly in* PAULA'S *face.*)   You *know* what I mean.

PAULA (*still clutching her*).   You accuse me!

ELLEAN.   It's in your face!

PAULA (*hoarsely*).   You—you think I'm—that sort of creature, do you?

ELLEAN.   Let me go!

PAULA.   Answer me!   You've always hated me!   (*Shaking her.*)   Out with it!

ELLEAN.   You hurt me!

PAULA.   You've always hated me!   You shall answer me!

ELLEAN.   Well, then, I have always—always——

PAULA.   What?

ELLEAN.   I have always known what you were!

PAULA.   Ah! (*She releases her and feebly grasps back of* L.C. *chair.*)   Who—who told you?

ELLEAN.   Nobody but yourself.   From the first moment I saw you I knew you were altogether unlike the good women I'd left; directly I saw you I knew what my father had done.   You've wondered why I've turned from you!   There—that's the reason!   Oh, but this is a horrible way for the truth to come home to every one! Oh! (*She moves down* R.C.)

PAULA (*madly*).   It's a lie!   It's all a lie! (*Forcing* ELLEAN *down upon her knees.*)   You shall beg my pardon for it.

(ELLEAN *utters a loud shriek of terror.*)

Ellean, I'm a good woman!   I swear I am!   I've always been a good woman!   You dare to say I've ever been anything else! (*Throwing her off violently.*)   It's a lie!

(AUBREY *re-enters.*)

AUBREY.   Paula!

(PAULA *staggers back up* C. *to* R.C. *window.* AUBREY *advances. Raising* ELLEAN.)

What's this?   What's this?

ELLEAN (*faintly*).   Nothing. (*She goes round the ottoman and leans upon it.*)   It—it's my fault.   Father, I—I don't wish to see Captain Ardale again.

(*She goes out door* R., AUBREY *slowly following her to the door.*)

PAULA.   Aubrey, she—she guesses.

AUBREY.   Guesses?

PAULA.   About me—and Ardale.

AUBREY. About you—and Ardale ?

PAULA. She says she suspected my character from the beginning . . . that's why she's always kept me at a distance . . . and now she sees through——

(*She falters ; he helps her to the ottoman* R.C., *where she sits.*)

AUBREY (*bending over her*). Paula, you must have said something—admitted something——

PAULA. I don't think so. It—it's in my face.

AUBREY. What ?

PAULA. She tells me so. She's right ! I'm tainted through and through ; anybody can see it, anybody can find it out. You said much the same to me to-night.

AUBREY (*partly to himself, as if dazed*). If she has got this idea into her head we must drive it out, that's all. We must take steps to—— What shall we do ? We had better—better—— (*Sitting* L.C. *and staring before him.*) What—what ?

PAULA (*lifting her head, after a pause*). Ellean ! So meek, so demure ! You've often said she reminded you of her mother. Yes, I know now what your first marriage was like.

AUBREY (*as before*). We must drive this idea out of her head. We'll do something. What shall we do ?

PAULA. She's a regular woman too. She could forgive *him* easily enough—but *me* ! That's just a woman !

AUBREY. What *can* we do ?

PAULA. Why, nothing ! She'd have no difficulty in following up her suspicions. Suspicions ! You should have seen how she looked at me !

(*He buries his head in his hands. There is silence for a time, then she rises slowly, crosses to* L.C., *takes chair from behind table and sits beside him.*)

Aubrey !

AUBREY. Yes.

(*She looks at him pityingly.*)

PAULA (*moving slightly*). I'm very sorry.

(*Without meeting her eyes, he lays his hand on her arm for a moment.*)

AUBREY (*rousing himself*). Well, we must look things straight in the face. (*Glancing round.*) At any rate, we've done with this.

PAULA (*following his glance*). I suppose so. (*After a brief pause.*) Of course, she and I can't live under the same roof any more. (*Abruptly.*) You know she kissed me to-night, of her own accord.

AUBREY. I asked her to alter towards you.

PAULA (*disappointed*). That was it, then.

AUBREY. I—I'm sorry I sent her away.

PAULA. It was my fault ; I made it necessary.

AUBREY. Perhaps now she'll propose to return to the convent,
—well, she must.

PAULA. Would you like to keep her with you and—and leave
me ?

AUBREY. Paula——!

PAULA. You needn't be afraid I'd go back to—what I was. I
couldn't.

AUBREY. Sssh, for God's sake ! We—you and I—we'll get out
of this place . . . what a fool I was to come here again !

PAULA. You lived here with your first wife !

AUBREY. We'll get out of this place and go abroad again, and
begin afresh.

PAULA. Begin afresh ?

AUBREY. There's no reason why the future shouldn't be happy
for us—no reason that I can see—— (*Almost discussing his own
helplessness.*)

PAULA (*abruptly*). Aubrey !

AUBREY. Yes ?

PAULA (*matter of fact*). You'll never forget this, you know.

AUBREY. This ?

PAULA. To-night, and everything that's led up to it. Our
coming here, Ellean, our quarrels—cat and dog !—Mrs. Cortelyon,
the Orreyeds, this man ! What an everlasting nightmare for you !

AUBREY. Oh, we can forget it, if we choose.

PAULA. That was always your cry. How *can* one do it ?

AUBREY. We'll make our calculations solely for the future, talk
about the future, think about the future.

PAULA. I believe the future is only the past again, entered
through another gate.

AUBREY. That's an awful belief.

PAULA. To-night proves it. You must see now that, do what
we will, go where we will, you'll be continually reminded of—what
I was. I see it.

AUBREY. You're frightened to-night ; meeting this man has
frightened you. But that sort of thing isn't likely to recur. The
world isn't quite so small as all that.

PAULA. Isn't it ! The only great distances it contains are those
we carry within ourselves—the distances that separate husbands and
wives, for instance. And so it'll be with us. You'll do your best—
oh, I know that—you're a good fellow. But circumstances will be
too strong for you in the end, mark my words.

AUBREY. Paula——!

PAULA. Of course I'm pretty now—I'm pretty still—and a pretty
woman, whatever else she may be, is always—well, endurable. But
even now I notice that the lines of my face are getting deeper ; so
are the hollows about my eyes. Yes, my face is covered with little
shadows that usen't to be there. Oh, I know I'm " going off." I
hate paint and dye and those messes, but, by and by, I shall drift

the way of the others ; I shan't be able to help myself. And then, some day—perhaps very suddenly, under a queer, fantastic light at night or in the glare of the morning—that horrid, irresistible truth that physical repulsion forces on men and women will come to you, and you'll sicken at me.

AUBREY.   I——!

PAULA (*she delivers this speech staring forward, as if she were looking at what she describes*).   You'll see me then, at last, with other people's eyes ; you'll see me just as your daughter does now, as all wholesome folks see women like me. And I shall have no weapon to fight with—not one serviceable little bit of prettiness left me to defend myself with ! A worn-out creature—broken up, very likely, some time before I ought to be—my hair bright, my eyes dull, my body too thin or too stout, my cheeks raddled and ruddled—a ghost, a wreck, a caricature, a candle that gutters, call such an end what you like ! Oh, Aubrey, what shall I be able to say to you then ? And this is the future you talk about ! I know it—I know it !

(*He is still sitting staring forward ; she rocks herself to and fro as if in pain.*)

Oh, Aubrey ! Oh ! Oh !

(*With a long, low wail she bends forward till her head almost touches her knees. He tries to comfort her. She straightens herself and lays her head upon his shoulder.*)

AUBREY.   Paula——!

PAULA (*with a moan*).   Oh, and I wanted so much to sleep to-night !

(*From the distance, in the garden L., there comes the sound of DRUM-MLE'S voice ; he is singing as he approaches the house.*)

(*Listening.*)   That's Cayley, coming back from The Warren. (*Starting up.*)   He doesn't know, evidently. I—I won't see him !

(*She goes out quickly, door R. DRUMMLE'S voice comes nearer. By a strong effort AUBREY rouses himself and rises. For a moment he stands C., irresolute ; then an idea comes to him. He puts the chair that PAULA has used back behind the table, snatches up a book, and sitting on settee L. makes a pretence of reading. After a moment or two, DRUMMLE appears at the window L.C. and looks in.*)

DRUMMLE.   Aha ! my dear chap !

AUBREY.   Cayley ?

DRUMMLE (*coming into the room*).   I went down to The Warren after you.

AUBREY.   Yes ?

DRUMMLE.   Missed you. Well ? I've been gossiping with Mrs. Cortelyon. (*Removing a handkerchief which he has tied round his throat.*)   Confound you, I've heard the news !

AUBREY (*lowering his book*).   What have you heard ?

DRUMMLE.   What have I heard ! Why—Ellean and young

Ardale ! (*Checking himself—looking at* AUBREY *keenly.*) My dear
Aubrey ! Alice is under the impression that you are inclined to
look on the affair favourably.

AUBREY (*rising and advancing to* DRUMMLE). You've not—met
Captain Ardale ? (*Puts the book on the table.*)

DRUMMLE. No. Why do you ask ? (*Hesitatingly.*) By the by,
I don't know that I need tell you—but it's rather strange. He's
not at The Warren to-night.

AUBREY. No ?

DRUMMLE (*quickly and lightly*). He left the house half an hour
ago, to stroll about the lanes ; just now a note came from him, a
scribble in pencil, simply telling Alice that she would receive a letter
from him to-morrow. What's the matter ? There's nothing very
wrong, is there ? My dear chap, pray forgive me if I'm asking too
much.

AUBREY. Cayley, you—you urged me to send her away !

DRUMMLE. Ellean ! Yes, yes. But—but—by all accounts this
is quite an eligible young fellow. Alice has been giving me the
history——

AUBREY (*madly*). Curse him ! (*Hurling his book to the floor.*)
Curse him ! Yes, I do curse him—him and his class ! Perhaps I
curse myself too in doing it. He has only led " a man's life "—just
as I, how many of us, have done ! The misery he has brought on
me and mine it's likely enough we, in our time, have helped to bring
on others by this leading " a man's life " ! But I do curse him for
all that. My God, *I've* nothing more to fear—I've paid *my* fine !
And so I can curse him in safety. Curse him ! Curse him !

DRUMMLE. In Heaven's name, tell me what's happened ?

AUBREY (*gripping* DRUMMLE's *arm*). Paula ! Paula !

DRUMMLE. What ?

AUBREY. They met to-night here. They—they—they're not
strangers to each other.

DRUMMLE. Aubrey ! (*He moves slowly up* C.)

AUBREY. Curse him ! My poor, wretched wife ! My poor,
wretched wife ! (*He sinks into* L.C. *chair.*)

(*The door* R. *opens and* ELLEAN *appears. The two men turn to her.
There is a moment's silence.*)

ELLEAN (*very quietly*). Father . . . father . . . !

AUBREY. Ellean ?

ELLEAN. I—I want you. (*He goes to her.*) Father . . . go to
Paula ! (*He looks into her face, startled.*) Quickly—quickly !
(*He passes her to go out, she seizes his arm, with a cry.*) No, no ;
don't go !

(*He shakes her off and goes.* ELLEAN *staggers back towards* DRUMMLE.)

DRUMMLE (*to* ELLEAN). What do you mean ? What do you
mean ?

ELLEAN. I—I went to her room—to tell her I was sorry for something I had said to her. And I *was* sorry—I *was* sorry. I heard the fall. I—I've seen her. It's horrible.

DRUMMLE. She—she has——!

ELLEAN. Killed—herself? (*Nodding.*) Yes—yes. So everybody will say. But I know—I helped to kill her. If I had only been merciful! (*She beats her breast.*)

(*She faints upon the ottoman. He pauses for a moment irresolutely— then he goes to the door R., opens it, and stands looking off.*)

CURTAIN.

PROPERTY PLOT

ACT I

See description of Scene, also Ground Plan.
Cigar-cutter on table L.O.
Paper-knife on writing-table.
Three hats and three coats for MORSE.
Salver and letters for MORSE.
Letter, flowers and cloak for PAULA.

ACT II

See description of Scene, also Ground Plan.
Flowers for PAULA on table R.O.
Three letters for AUBREY on table L.O.
Dishes for SERVANTS off O.
Flowers and sprig of gorse for ELLMAN.
Lady Orreyed's letter.
Newspaper.

ACT III

See description of Scene, also Ground Plan.
Bottle of smelling-salts.
Piece of good delicate china on table L.O.
Tray and coffee-cups for SERVANT.
Three unopened stamped letters for PAULA.
Rose for HUGH.

ACT IV

Same as Act III.
Small chair down L. brought to back of table L.O.
Cigar for DRUMMLE.
Salver and written letter for SERVANT.

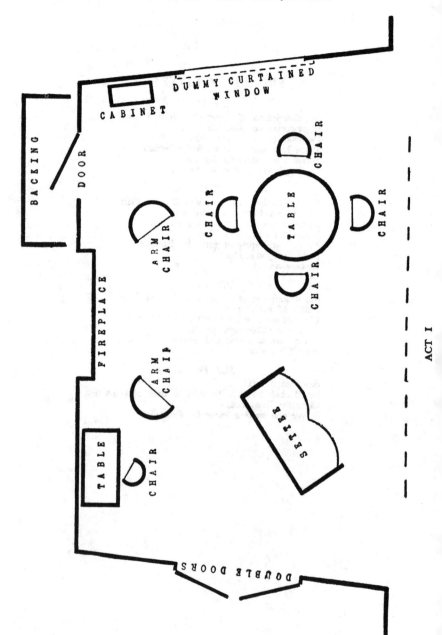

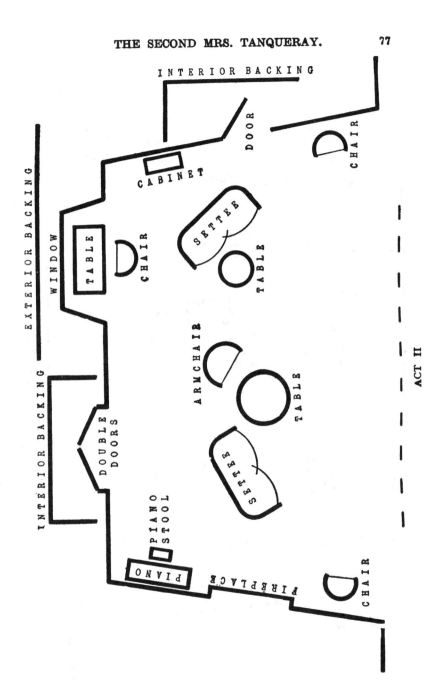

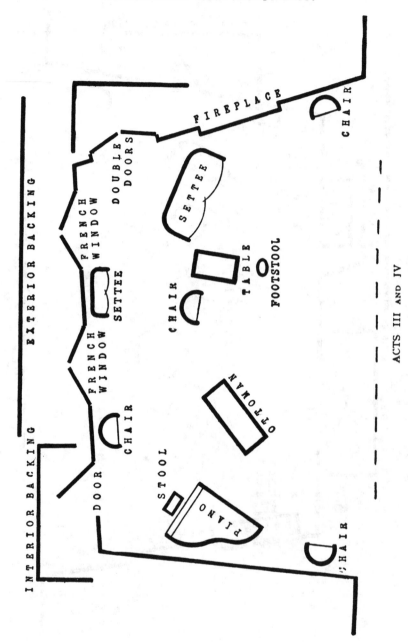

ACTS III and IV